Historic Homes

of

FLORIDA'S
FIRST COAST

Historic Homes

of

FLORIDA'S
FIRST COAST

MARY ATWOOD
with WILLIAM WEEKS

THE
History
PRESS

Published by The History Press
Charleston, SC 29403
www.historypress.net

Cover images are original photographs by Mary Atwood.

First published 2014

Manufactured in the United States

ISBN 978.1.62619.726.8

Library of Congress CIP data applied for.

This book is dedicated to my son, Christopher David Atwood, whose great love of history I share, and whose formidable command of the subject matter I continually strive to match.

Although I have taken on many tasks in my lifetime and enjoyed a certain amount of success at most of them, whatever part I played in the cultivation of his character will always be my proudest accomplishment.

CONTENTS

CONTENTS

FOREWORD

M uch of the history of a place is told by the colorful characters who once lived there.

Although they are now long gone, their personalities live on in the homes they have left behind, the palpable remnants of lives lived large.

Their homes are like a portal through time that takes us back to the daily ebb and flow of life, the intimate rooms where their dreams were made, the panes of wavy glass through which they looked out upon their world and the poignant everyday furnishings of a simpler time.

Fewer and fewer homes remain from over one hundred years ago, and those that still exist can transport us through layers of time to connect us with the inhabitants of a distant world, a world that has now become the place we live today.

The homes that have survived decades and centuries are tangible reminders of this past, and in this book they become characters in a larger story that spans a significant part of Florida's history as well as a large swath of the top-right corner of this colorful state.

Too often the "story" is missing from the word "history." But, with a storyteller's flair for description, a historian's dedication to research and a photographer's eye for detail, Mary Atwood connects all of these colorful people and places in a very memorable fashion. She distills the chronology and the layers of history in a way that the reader can easily understand the timeline of Northeast Florida's past. Equally important, she provides both historical and personal images that give us greater appreciation for the significant people and buildings depicted in this book.

Historic Homes of Florida's First Coast takes us from the primitive homes of St. Augustine's early Spanish settlers to the Florida Cracker home of author Marjorie Kinnan Rawlings at Cross Creek. It guides us through almost two centuries of historic homes and is a testimonial to the richness of the older architecture of Florida (a state that is often dismissed as having only a superficial and recent heritage).

The photographs included in this book help us see the textures and find the feeling of a particular time and place in history. Many of the photographic vignettes taken by the author go beyond mere pictorial description. They are truly works of art and stand as silent portraits of the past that crystallize moments long gone.

Mary Atwood's talents as a communicator stem from her childhood. She has vivid memories of sitting on her grandfather's knee in a creaky old metal rocking chair on the front porch of his log cabin in the hills of southern Tennessee. Young Mary was entranced by his stories of the characters and places in the rural Southern community. That house (which she affectionately calls "PawPaw's Farm") was a typical nineteenth-century simple, one-story cabin made of logs chinked with mortar. But in the eyes of a little girl, it was a vast and mysterious place that smelled of ancient wood and whose dimly lit nooks and crannies were the hiding places for untold memories. To this day, memories of that log cabin resonate with her as the place she felt most at home.

Her father grew up in this cabin, and he later became a navy photographer. His talents flowed through to Mary, who, at age six, began her lifelong affection for photography with her family's Kodak Brownie. At age ten, she got the first camera of her own—a Polaroid Swinger. She took a photo of her cat and sent the image to Polaroid to get an eight-by-ten-inch enlargement made and had it framed. When she was thirteen, she got her first 35 mm camera. She knew at age sixteen she wanted to be a professional photographer, and by the time she was twenty, she owned a Hasselblad, the *ne plus ultra* of cameras at the time.

Throughout her life, Mary has felt that her camera is an extension of not only her eyes but also of her heart. In her words, she is "an artist, an observer and a visual communicator. My primary medium is photography, though I have always been a writer as well."

Mary relished the idea of taking on the project of creating this book, which coalesces her love of writing, photography, history and storytelling.

The author's father and aunt in front of the log cabin at her "PawPaw's Farm" in 1943.

Her exploration of Florida's First Coast has been a journey of personal discovery that she has generously shared with us. This book is a valuable contribution to the understanding of Northeast Florida's history.

—Dr. Wayne W. Wood, Hon. AIA
Author of *Jacksonville's Architectural Heritage: Landmarks for the Future*

PREFACE

The writing of this book is the end result of an art project entitled First Coast Reflections, which I began creating, quite by accident, in 2011. The story begins with a single image, captured in a serendipitous moment.

I was delivering artwork to a show in Gainesville early on a Saturday morning in 2009 and had a friend riding along to keep me company. On the way, she asked if I had ever been to the Dudley Farm State Park. I confessed that not only had I never been there, I had never even heard of Dudley Farm. My friend explained to me that it was an old homestead from the 1800s, which had been converted into a state park and kept operating as a working farm. Intrigued, I agreed that we would go when my delivery had been completed.

We arrived at the farm later that day and walked the small dirt path that leads to the farmhouse, making our way through the dense pine forest. Upon first sight of the house, I couldn't help but feel somewhat disappointed. The small structure looked unimpressive from the outside—built of unpainted wood siding; situated in the center of the yard, which had a few flowers but was completely barren of grass; and surrounded by a simply constructed cattle wire fence. Somehow I had imagined something more, although I had no idea what.

But as I passed through the screen door, I entered a world that would eventually speak to me of more than one lost childhood memory. A door in the kitchen that had been left slightly ajar led me to a small pantry area with open shelves bearing stacks of white dishes and clear glasses gleaming in the sunshine spilling in from a nearby window. In front of that window was an old ironing board covered with a well-worn bedsheet. I remember briefly thinking that the scene had a very familiar feel to it, so I photographed it and then moved on to the next room without giving it much thought. I photographed several of the outbuildings, watched spellbound as a young man cooked cane syrup and spent a few minutes visiting with the farm's mule. I never pass up an opportunity to make a new equine friend. While I enjoyed my visit to the farm, I certainly didn't leave with the impression that something magical had just happened.

It wasn't until I arrived home and transferred the day's images from the camera to the computer that I realized the personal significance of the pantry scene. Staring at the image on my monitor, my mind began to replay short scenes of long forgotten memories…of white dishes in my mother's kitchen cabinets, of learning to iron on a board covered with an old sheet, of visits to the farmhouse where my grandfather lived when I was a very young child. I became acutely aware of the ability of that image to communicate on a deep and intimate level and suddenly found myself fighting back tears.

"Comfort," from the First Coast Reflections project, Dudley Farm. *Author's original image.*

It was at that moment that First Coast Reflections was conceived as an art project: to locate and document historically significant, yet intimate, settings that speak of our collective past.

Almost as soon as I started the research process, I became acutely aware of the enormous amount of time, effort and financial resources that would be required to successfully complete the task I had assigned for myself. Realizing that I would need to find an additional source for funding, I naively applied for only one grant. Fortunately, the grant selection committee of the Community Foundation in Jacksonville understood and appreciated my vision and selected me as the recipient of an Art Ventures Grant in 2011. I soon began spending every spare moment working to produce what eventually became a collection of thirty-two original, large black-and-white photographic prints for exhibition.

The process of researching appropriate locations, arranging visits to historic sites, gaining permission to take photographs, cataloguing images captured and then selecting and preparing those that most clearly spoke of the message I wanted to share consumed well over two years of my life. Booking, delivering and installing exhibitions of the collection began in January of 2012 and continues to this day.

The project has been a labor of love and an effort to share the profound respect I have for those who helped to create the history of this area. The difficulties they encountered and overcame transformed the simple acts of everyday living into extraordinary expressions of faith, courage and love. And in some cases, their struggles produced long-enduring music and literature, which are easily capable of moving me to tears.

In following the journeys of these early settlers, I unknowingly embarked on one of my own, which eventually led me across the Atlantic Ocean to share my photographic collection with the citizens of Jacksonville's sister city of Nantes, France. During my flight to Paris, I couldn't help but reflect on the fact that I was crossing over the same waters the early settlers so bravely sailed in their small ships to settle the then-unexplored land I now call home.

At the time, I thought that the exhibition in Nantes might be the culmination of the First Coast Reflections project—perhaps a "full circle" of sorts and a fitting end. But it seems it was only a pause in the journey, a detour on the way to the next destination, which was unknown at the time. That next destination was the writing of this book.

So as the journey continues, I invite you to join me in exploring the people, places and stories of some of the historic homes of Florida's First Coast.

Acknowledgements

There are many individuals and organizations whose contributions to this project I would like to gratefully acknowledge. It is only right that I begin with the Community Foundation in Jacksonville, which awarded the Art Ventures Grant that made it possible for me to create the First Coast Reflections photography project, which has served as the foundation for this book.

I would also like to thank the following organizations for so generously sharing the stories of the people and places featured in this book and allowing me to photograph the locations included. In many cases, special permission was granted.

Thank you to Ranger Crystal Jackson; the staff of the Kingsley Plantation; the National Park Service; Sandy Arpen; the staff of the Major Webb House Museum; the Mandarin Historical Society; Dr. Derek Hall; Jacksonville University; Emily Retherford Lisska; Dr. Wayne Wood; the staff of the Merrill House Museum; the Jacksonville Historical Society; Taryn Rodríguez-Boette; Joshua T. Edwards; Lee McDonald; the staff of the Beaches Museum and History Park; the Beaches Area Historical Society; the Sisters of St. Joseph of St. Augustine; the staff of the Father Miguel O'Reilly House Museum; Dr. Susan Parker; Jeanette Vigliotti; the staff of the Oldest House Museum Complex; the St. Augustine Historical Society; Doris Wiles; Margo Pope; Ann Myers; the staff of the Pena Peck House Museum; the Woman's Exchange of St. Augustine; Julia Vaill Gatlin; the staff of the Ximenez-Fatio House Museum; the National Society of the Colonial Dames of America in the State of Florida; Andrew Sandall; Roy Shaffer; Melissa Stuart; the staff of the Dow Museum of Historical Houses; the Museum of Arts and Sciences, Daytona Beach; Carolyn Day; Cindy Cheatwood; the staff of the Clarke House Museum; the Orange Park Historical Society; Rick Mulligan; the staff of the Marjorie Kinnan Rawlings Historic State Park; and the Florida State Parks System.

Additionally, I would like to thank my parents—my mother, Earline Anderson, who taught me to believe in my dreams and my father, Charles Woy, who taught me the value of hard work. I would also like to thank Chuck and Tracy Woy, who have carried my share of the family responsibilities in more ways than I can count.

I must also express my tremendous gratitude to Rick Atwood, Gene Atwood and Patricia Atwood. Their steadfast support has continuously provided me with the opportunity to pursue my dreams. And, of course, I would like to thank Christopher Atwood, who is my daily inspiration.

I also want to acknowledge and thank my friends, who have supported me in many ways throughout this process. Those who deserve special thanks for their assistance are my friend Bob Hunt for his generous support of the First Coast Reflections project and consistent faith in my abilities; my good friend and business partner, Jim Smith, for his invaluable advice and endless encouragement; my coauthor and best friend of many years, Bill Weeks, for agreeing to share his amazing talents in this adventure; and my friend Dr. Wayne Wood, who has provided me with excellent advice and has generously agreed to write the foreword and was the first person to suggest the idea of expanding the First Coast Reflections fine art photography project into the book you are now reading.

Additionally, I would like to thank the members of the Art Center Cooperative, the Jacksonville Artists Guild and the Artists Guild of Orange Park for their kindness, support and for providing infinite opportunities for artistic growth. Special thanks to my friend and fellow artist, Leigh Murphy, for introducing me to the Dudley Farm in Newberry, where this journey began.

Finally, I would like to express my gratitude to Leigh Rodante and the Ponte Vedra Cultural Center; Meredith Fordham Hughes and the JaxPort Gallery; Christy Leonard and the Museum of Science and History in Jacksonville; Rick Minor and the Karpeles Museum of Jacksonville; Tony Walsh and the Thrasher Horne Center for the Arts in Orange Park; Jack Matthews and the Schultz Center for Teaching and Leadership; Allie Gloe and the Haskell Gallery at Jacksonville International Airport; Pamela Beaton and the

Jacksonville Public Library; Mollie Doctrow and the Museum of Florida Art and Culture in Avon Park, Florida; Lisa Thompson and the Hardee Center for the Arts at the North Florida Community College, Madison, Florida; Dr. Joanne Davis and the Jacksonville Sister Cities Association; Sheila Kloc and L'Alliance Française de Jacksonville; Mariette Cassourret and the Seattle-Nantes-Jacksonville Association; Eva Prevost, the cultural and consular specialist at the United States embassy in Rennes, France; and Robert Tate, consul for the United States for western France. It is only through the experiences associated with the exhibitions hosted by these individuals and their organizations that I found the inspiration to write this book.

INTRODUCTION

The First Coast area of Florida is so named because of both its location and its history. It lies on the eastern coast of the peninsula, just south of the Georgia border, and is the first area encountered by visitors from the north arriving via Interstate 95.

It is also where the construction of Fort Caroline took place more than forty years prior to the attempted settlement of Jamestown in Virginia and more than fifty years before the landing of the *Mayflower* at Plymouth Rock.

It is an area in which three European colonial powers fought for control more than four hundred years ago and lost many of their bravest men in the process. It is an area where the efforts of early settlers to carve out an existence were repeatedly tested by both raging fires and bitter freezes. It is an area whose history has been built on courage and determination. And at the heart of the First Coast area is the city of Jacksonville.

Jacksonville, which incorporates all of Duval County, is located on the northeast Atlantic coast of Florida and is divided by the north-flowing St. Johns River. As the largest city in land area among the lower forty-eight states, it offers a diverse topography including barrier islands, salt marshes and estuaries and a surprisingly large area of still undeveloped forests. In the developed areas, one can easily spot bottle-nosed dolphins swimming in the St. Johns River and, in the warm months of summer, the endangered Florida manatees. From the tops of the city's bridges, the smaller buildings of the suburban areas disappear beneath the expansive canopy of old-growth oak trees and scrub pines. Bald eagles, osprey, herons, egrets and

The skyline of downtown Jacksonville. *Author's original image.*

roseate spoonbills build their nests in these trees and are often found along the banks of the waterways.

The City of Jacksonville operates the largest urban park system in the United States, which is supplemented by ten additional parks owned by the State of Florida, as well as the Timucuan Ecological and Historic Preserve, which is operated by the United States National Park Service.

Jacksonville's beauty can also be found in its history. Contained within the Timucuan Preserve is the Kingsley Plantation, the oldest residential structure in the city of Jacksonville and the oldest surviving plantation home in Florida.

Although much of Jacksonville's downtown area was lost in the Great Fire of 1901, the 1886 Merrill House survived the massive destruction and now stands as one of the city's most important historic landmarks. Additionally, historic districts are found in the suburbs of Springfield, Riverside, Avondale, Ortega and San Marco.

Still within the confines of Jacksonville city limits, but approximately fifteen miles south of the downtown area on the eastern banks of the St. Johns River, is the community of Mandarin. Here, the steamships of the late nineteenth century made daily stops to take on fruit from the groves of oranges owned by Major Webb.

Slightly south of Major Webb's groves, a young Englishman named Frederick Delius lived for eighteen months in a small home on a plantation known as Solano Grove. He deferred the responsibilities of tending his groves to hired hands so that he could devote all of his time to his musical education.

East of the city of Jacksonville lies the Atlantic Ocean and the beach communities. Jacksonville Beach was once connected to the city by railway. Even though the railroad no longer exists, the Foreman's House built in 1900 still stands just a short distance from its original location.

Along the coast to the south of Jacksonville's beaches, partially protected from fierce Atlantic storms by Anastasia Island, lies the "ancient city" of St. Augustine. Founded by the Spanish in 1565, the city's "Old Town" section has long been recognized as a historic treasure and contains numerous homes of historic significance, as well as a unique architectural style that grew from the cultural diversity of its history.

Crossing the St. Johns River to its western banks directly opposite the community of Mandarin lies the city of Orange Park. A rural area until the mid-twentieth century, early area settlers William and Carrie Clarke bought property there to provide their only son with ample opportunities to have a more "wholesome" childhood than he would experience in the nearby city of Jacksonville.

Further inland is the Gainesville area, a once-rural community that became home to the University of Florida in 1905. Just to the west of the city, in the nearby community of Newberry, the Dudley family operated a highly successful farm for more than one hundred years. To the southeast of Gainesville, nestled between Orange and Lochloosa Lakes, is an area known as Cross Creek. There, Florida's most treasured writer, Marjorie Kinnan Rawlings, wrote her masterpiece, the universally appealing coming-of-age story *The Yearling*.

These are the people and the places whose stories are told in *Historic Homes of Florida's First Coast*. They were the early settlers who left behind friends, family and familiar surroundings to build new lives in a primitive wilderness. They were men who toiled in fields to coax crops from soil that consists largely of sand. They were women who started each day by stoking the fires of their wood-burning stoves in sweltering kitchens in order to feed their families. They were the musicians and artists and writers who captured and celebrated the spirit of the land and its people in works that have timeless appeal. Their individual and collective actions, both ordinary and extraordinary, played an important part in shaping our past and continue to provide us with the inspiration to forge our own futures in the area known as Florida's First Coast.

JACKSONVILLE

The first Europeans to attempt settlement in this area were the French Protestant Huguenots who fled their homeland to seek refuge from religious persecution in their native France. Under the leadership of Jean Ribault, 150 settlers boarded two ships and sailed from the French port of Le Havre in February 1562. On the first day of May, Ribault sailed his ships up what is now known as the St. Johns River, where he ordered a stone column to be erected to claim the land for France. He named the waterway *Riviere de Mai* (River of May) in honor of the day he first sailed upon its waters. This brief visit to the area was followed by an attempt at settlement in South Carolina, which ended in failure.

Two years later, a second settlement under the leadership of René Goulaine de Laudonnière initially appeared to hold more promise of success. He arrived on June 22, 1564, with two hundred French Huguenot settlers and received an additional one hundred reinforcements with the return of Jean Ribault the following year. This expedition saw the founding of Fort Caroline on a high bluff along the St. Johns River.

Laudonnière said of the site:

> *Nowe was I determined to search out the qualities of the hill. Therefore I went right to the toppe thereof, where we found nothing else but Cedars, Palme, and Baytrees of so souereigne odour, that Baulme smelleth nothing like in comparison. The trees were enuironed* [sic] *rounde about with Vines bearing grapes in such quantitie, that the number would suffice to make the*

place habitable. Besides this fertilitie of the soyle for Vines, a man may see Esquine wreathed about the shrubs in great quantitie. Touching the pleasure of the place, the Sea may be seene plaine and open from it, and more then sixe leagues off, neere the Riuer Belle, a man may behold the medowes diuided asunder into Iles and Islets enterlacing one another: Briefly the place is so pleasant, that those which are melancholicke would be enforced to change their humour.[1]

Yet, the "pleasure of the place" would prove to be short lived for the French settlers. The first battle between rival settlers in the New World would take place at Fort Caroline a mere three months after their arrival.

Spanish soldiers under the command of Pedro Menéndez, who had established a small settlement in St. Augustine just a few weeks before, mounted a surprise attack on the French fort at sunrise on the morning of September 20, 1565. Unfortunately, the fort was almost completely undefended, as most of the French soldiers had set sail for the Spanish settlement of St. Augustine ten days earlier under the command of the recently returned Jean Ribault. Laudonnière later recorded in his report to the King of France:

Perceiving the great extremity of the situation, I reviewed the men left to me by Captain Ribault to see how many of them could bear arms. I found nine or ten, but I believe that no more than two or three had ever drawn a sword. Among those who say that there were sufficient persons to defend the fort, they should listen, and observe the men who were there. Of the nine, four were youths who served Captain Ribault in taking care of his dogs. The fifth was a cook.[2]

Additionally, the soldiers who had been assigned to stand watch at the fort on the night of the nineteenth were allowed by their commander to retire for the night because of a storm so violent that it was incorrectly presumed that the Spanish would not attempt an attack under such terrible conditions.

The battle at Fort Caroline lasted less than an hour, and when it was over, 140 French settlers had lost their lives. Soldiers who survived the battle were hanged with an inscribed sign posted above them, which read, "I do this, not as to Frenchmen, but as to Lutherans." The Protestant Bibles and symbols of Huguenot faith were burned. The scene was described by a surviving carpenter, Nicolas Le Challeux, who escaped to the nearby forest:

From this place all the fort, even the inner court was distinctly visible to me, looking there I saw a horrible butchery of our men taking place and three standards of our enemies planted upon the ramparts. Having then lost all hope of seeing our men rally, I resigned my senses to the Lord.[3]

Fewer than fifty of the French colonists survived the attack. Included among them was Laudonnière, who escaped the fort and, according to his own account of the events, "spent that night in water up to my shoulders, along with one of my men who would never leave me."[4]

Those who had been fortunate enough to escape the carnage that took place at Fort Caroline quickly set sail for France. They departed on September 25, thus ending the first European settlement in the Jacksonville area after a period of only 455 days.

The Spanish took control of the fort and renamed it San Matteo. They also renamed the river *Rio de San Juan* (St. Johns River) after the San Juan del Puerto mission they had established at the river's mouth. The Spanish settlement would be short lived, as the fort would be burned to the ground by French troops led by Dominique de Gourgues in 1568.

Gourgues was a French nobleman who had been captured by the Spanish as a young boy and forced to work as a galley slave. Although he eventually escaped, his dislike for the Spanish increased with age. When he heard of the events at Fort Caroline, he sold enough of his own personal belongings to outfit three small ships and finance a voyage to Spanish Florida. Upon his arrival, he led his own men and a contingent of friendly natives in a raid on Fort San Matteo. While most of the Spanish soldiers were killed, those who were captured were hung, just as the Spanish had hung the French they captured three years earlier. An inscription was left, which read, "This is done, not as unto Spaniards, but as unto liars, thieves, and murderers."[5]

Although the Spanish rebuilt the fort almost immediately, they chose to abandon it the following year. So neither the French nor the Spanish settlers were responsible for the settlement of the area that would become Jacksonville.

The establishment of the city actually traces its history back to the construction of the "Kings Road" by the British after Florida was ceded by the Spanish in 1763. Over three thousand Spanish residents of Florida were unwilling to live under English rule and left for Cuba and Mexico. By the time the British assumed control, there were only three families remaining in St. Augustine and the surrounding areas, which Governor James Grant characterized as a "New World in a State

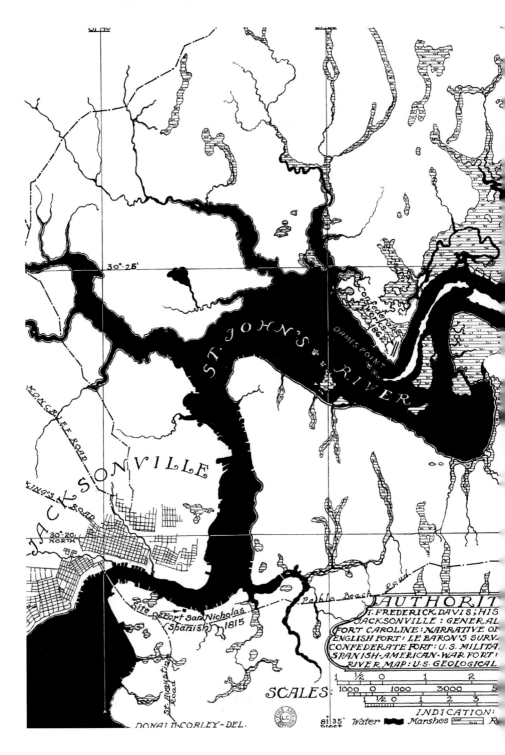

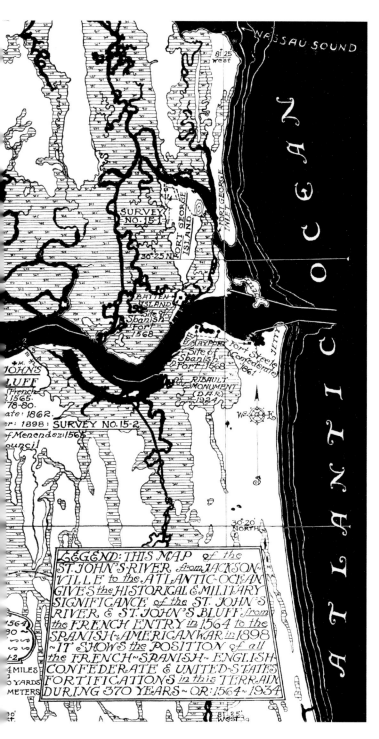

A 1930s map of the Jacksonville area, indicating the previous locations of French and Spanish forts, St. John's Bluff and Fort George Island. *Courtesy of the Library of Congress.*

of Nature." Hoping to lure settlers from the northern colonies, the new governor ordered the construction of a road that would cover the 106-mile distance between the coastal village of New Smyrna in Florida and the town of Colerain in the colony of Georgia.

The road, which incorporated the trails of Native Americans, was laid out by John William Gerard de Brahm, a German-born cartographer who had been appointed as surveyor general for the Georgia colony. East Florida's British lieutenant governor John Moultrie oversaw the road construction and personally laid out a route for the segment to run from St. Augustine north to the "cow-ford" (the current site of Jacksonville's Main Street Bridge), with Captain John Fairlamb and his nephew Joshua Yallowby supervising the work. What is now the downtown area of Jacksonville was, at that time, known only as the cow-ford because of a shallow narrowing in the St. Johns River that was used to drive cattle across the river.

When completed in 1775, the road measured sixteen feet wide, with ditches and simple pine log bridges over small creeks, causeways through the swamps, more substantially constructed bridges across the many creeks and ferries stationed at the St. Mary's and St. Johns Rivers. Although the surface was originally constructed with sand and crushed native coquina, stretches of the road were topped with oyster shells. In one area, near the San Sebastian River in St. Augustine, the contractors failed to remove the oysters from their shells, unintentionally providing a daily afternoon meal for flocks of buzzards and crows.

By 1775, due to the growing threat of revolution in the colonies and access provided by the new Kings Road, British loyalists began relocating to Florida, where unoccupied lands were made available for them.

King George II, hoping to inspire London investors to purchase large tracts of land in Florida, appointed John Bartram to the position of royal botanist and provided him with a stipend to explore the area in 1765. He and his son William traveled the waters of the St. Johns River for eight weeks, covering a distance of more than five hundred miles, and recorded their observation of soil quality, plants and trees in both written words and sketches.

William Bartram returned to the St. Johns again in 1773 for a second study of the river, which would last more than eight months. His journey was financed by the wealthy naturalist Dr. John Fothergill in exchange for the safe delivery of specimens gathered during the study. For this journey, Bartram acquired a small sailboat for the price of "three guineas" and equipped it with "a good sail, fishing tackle, a neat light fusee, powder and ball."[6]

In his book about the experience, he wrote of the St. Johns River and surrounding areas with great admiration:

> *Blessed land where the gods have amassed into one heap all the flowering plants, birds, fish and other wildlife of two continents in order to turn the rushing streams, the silent lake shores and the awe-abiding woodlands of this mysterious land into a true garden of Eden.*[7]

Of the land along the western banks of the St. Johns just south of the cow-ford where the Naval Air Station is now located, he wrote of being "struck with the magnificence of a venerable grove of Live Oaks, Palms, and Laurel (Magnolia Grandiflora). Orange trees were in full bloom, and filled the air with fragrance."[8]

East Florida under British rule would see the establishment of numerous plantations along the banks of the St. Johns River. Francis Philip Fatio managed the New Castle Plantation in the area now known as Arlington. Nearby were Captain William Reddy's Hampstead and Point Plantations. Samuel Potts purchased ten thousand acres for his Pottsburg Plantation on the land where the Arlington River meets the St. Johns. Philip Lee, who operated the ferry at the cow-ford, had a four-hundred-acre farm in the St. Nicolas area. James Box cleared one-fifth of his five-hundred-acre Hermitage Plantation, located in the San Marco area, for planting. Crops grown on the plantations included indigo, rice, corn, oranges and peaches.

Although the published works about the explorations of the Bartrams did accomplish the king's goal of exciting investors, the British planters would never be able to fully reap the rewards of their investments, since the 1783 Treaty of Versailles returned Florida to Spanish rule. The vast majority of the British settlers returned to England, though some moved to the newly formed United States. By 1784, only two plantations were still in operation.

The area was sparsely settled when the Spanish resumed control, so immigration policies were revised and new settlers began to arrive. But Spanish laws on trade and commerce were widely viewed by the settlers as too restrictive. In 1794, the Spanish militia burned a substantial amount of property north of the St. Johns River and placed five planters under arrest, including John McIntosh. Their arrests led to a short-lived rebellion in 1795, which laid the groundwork for a more intense and destructive uprising.

Due in large part to the combination of the events leading up to the 1795 rebellion and Spain's alliance with Britain, political leaders in Washington, D.C., grew anxious to see Florida become an American territory. In January

1811, a secret act for the acquisition was passed by Congress, which led to the outbreak of the Patriots Rebellion. With the assistance of the United States Navy, General George Matthews and the Patriots gained control of areas to the north of the St. Johns River, including the port of Fernandina. However, reports of the attack on Fernandina were not well received by either the populace of the United States or the Spanish government. The general opinion was that it was an unprovoked attack on a friendly colony. President Madison fired General Matthews, though word of his dismissal did not reach him until after his failed attempt to capture St. Augustine. In June 1812, the United States declared war on Britain, and President Madison abandoned all further efforts to claim Florida as a territory.

During the War of 1812, the British recruited Seminole warriors to fight alongside their soldiers. General Andrew Jackson invaded Spanish Florida in 1817 and attacked the tribe, pushing them out of the North Florida area. When Spain ceded Florida to the United States, efforts were made to relocate the Seminoles, as well as other tribes of the area, to the "Indian Territory" of what is now Oklahoma. Many refused and took their families south to establish the Seminole settlements in the Everglades, which still exist today.

It wasn't until the 1821 transfer of Florida to the United States that residents of the cow-ford area began to lay out formal plans for a nine-street town under the leadership of plantation owner Isaiah D. Hart. Hart had recently moved to the area, acquiring eighteen acres of land by trading cattle to Lewis Zachariah Hogans, who was the owner of more than two hundred acres he received in a Spanish land grant.

The original streets of the town were built in June 1822 on land donated by Hogans and another settler, John Brady. From the banks of the St. Johns River heading north, the original streets included Bay, Forsyth, Adams, Monroe and Duval. The streets that ran east to west were Washington, Liberty, Market and Newnan. The settlers decided to name their new city after Andrew Jackson, Florida's first territorial governor, although he never visited the city. The charter was approved in 1832.

Florida achieved statehood in 1837. Soon thereafter, the Jacksonville area saw a new influx of settlers, and the lumber business became the primary source of economic activity. By 1854, tourists were arriving in such numbers that boarding houses and fine hotels were being built in the city. Otis L. Keene, who was manager of the Judson House Hotel, wrote, "Orange groves were destroyed in the severe winter of 1835, yet the glory of the town was in its great stand of trees."[9]

Because roads were still insufficient for tourist travel, steamboats began offering sightseeing excursions on the St. Johns River. The schooners and other sail-powered vessels that dominated the maritime business along the coastline were often unable to enter Florida's inland waterways because of the constantly shifting sandbars found at their mouths.

Accounts of travel aboard the steamboats of the St. Johns River began to appear in the *New York Daily Times* in the 1850s, with writers describing the river as grand, majestic and surprisingly wide when compared to most northern rivers. But these pleasure journeys would soon be replaced by more serious activities, as the steamboats of the Union army entered the St. Johns River.

At the start of the Civil War, Jacksonville served as a key supply point for the Confederate cause. In September 1862, in an effort to curb the shipment of supplies to the Confederate army, the St. Johns River became the site of a Union blockade. The first occupation of Jacksonville by Union troops began in March 1862 and lasted approximately one month. However, the Union's naval fleet captured both Fernandina to the north and St. Augustine to the south, and established a base at Mayport Mills, located at the mouth of the St. Johns River.

Florida's economy at the time of the Civil War was based almost entirely on cattle and crops, and the state was also a major center of salt production, which was commonly used to preserve meat. Aside from the men who fought in the Civil War, Florida's greatest contribution was food supplies. Confederate soldiers were regularly assigned to the "Cow Cavalry" to carry out cattle raids to supply the troops with much-needed meat. One such soldier, who had been born in Duval County, was Jasper Jackson Dykes. He wrote about the importance of transporting beef and salt via the railroads, and his experience as a "cow-catcher" with the Second Cavalry, including a humorous observation regarding how much he was paid:

> *By the time of the 1860 census, I was 19 years old and the family had moved to Welaka, on the eastern shore of the St. Johns River, South of Palatka. When we moved there, my brother Elbert Duncan and I tried to make a living both as farmers and in the shipping industry that was thriving along the St. Johns River. At this time there were only two railroads that served the sparse population of the State of Florida. The Florida Atlantic & Gulf RR linked the St. Johns River port of Jacksonville to the tobacco and cotton plantations near Marianna in the panhandle of Florida. This railroad ran through the pine barrens of North Florida. It*

connected Jacksonville with the State Capital of Tallahassee, Monticello, Quincy, Madison, Lake City and Baldwin. There was a spur south out of Tallahassee that linked up the Gulf of Mexico at St. Marks.

The other railroad was called the Florida RR that was developed by David Levy Yulee. Yulee was the first man of Jewish faith to be elected to the U.S. Senate. The Florida RR connected the port of Fernandina with Cedar Key on the Gulf of Mexico. It ran through Micanopy, Gainesville, Waldo, Starke and Baldwin, where it connected to the Florida, Atlantic & Gulf RR. This route moved two important products, cattle and the salt to preserve it, to the ocean terminal.

On September 23, 1863, the 2nd Florida Cavalry was engaged in a skirmish at Magnolia, just north of Green Cove Springs. The end of September, the 2nd Florida Cavalry was again re-assigned to Cavalry, District of East Florida, Department of South Carolina, Georgia and Florida. I was paid again at $125.00, $30.00 for my equipment. I was detailed to the Commissary Department, spent the next 4 months as a "cow-catcher," helping to supply the Army of Northern Virginia with Florida beef. The South had to use Florida beef because when the Mississippi River was opened up to the Yankees, by the surrender of Vicksburg, it was more difficult to transport Texas beef to the rest of the Confederacy. The Yankee Navy was patrolling the Mississippi. A "cow-catcher" was the Palmetto Prairies answer to the Texas cowboy. For this same period, Major Teasdale paid me $122.00 for use and risk of my horse. I also got $45.00 for clothing on October 4, 1863. It didn't take me long to find out that my horse was worth more than I, as a soldier was worth.[10]

In the spring of 1863, Jacksonville was once again occupied by Union troops. Confederate general Joseph Finegan led an attack that drove the Union soldiers out of the city, but they set the city on fire as they retreated. An account in the *New York Herald-Tribune* described the destruction, writing that the city was "burned, scorched and crisped, if not entirely consumed to ashes, by the devouring flames."

By the end of the Civil War, the city had been occupied four different times and had been sacked by both Union and Confederate forces.

Shortly after the end of the war, the newly rebuilt city of Jacksonville was being billed as the "Winter City in Summer Land" and became a popular winter resort area. Grand hotels such as the St. James were open from January through April, providing elegant accommodations for wealthy visitors. The local souvenir shops featured alligator teeth fashioned into whistles, livery stables offered buggies and carriages for hire and there were boat excursions that took tourists as far upriver as Palatka.

A Vermont newspaper reporter named D. Webster Dixon wrote of his steamboat excursion on the St. Johns River in 1875:

> *I chose to take the steamer Dictator. At midnight we arrive at Fernandina (in Florida at the mouth of the St. Mary's River) where the captain preferred to remain for several hours for high tide to pass us over the bar, which in low water seriously obstructs the entrance to the St. Johns River. In the morning we saw the old abandoned lighthouse, large numbers of dolphins, and along the banks splendid specimens of oak, palmetto, and Magnolia.*[11]

A guidebook published in 1882 included the following description of the city:

> *There is in the city a quite remarkable number of handsome residences, and with very few exceptions they are surrounded by ample grounds laid out in tasteful gardens and lawns. Sometimes these gardens are perfect little parks, and the fruits, flowers, and shrubs all indicate a semi-tropical region. The society of Jacksonville is universally admitted to be unusually select, cultured, and refined; and the reasons are not far to seek. Many of the most prominent citizens have been drawn thither from all parts of the country on account of its climatic advantages, and are in general the picked men of their several localities. At any gathering of the best society there will be found gentlemen who have occupied high positions in all portions of the United States, and in nearly all professions and occupations—in the army, the navy, the judicial, the political, literary, artistic, and commercial world. As examples, I may mention that General Spinner, he of the famous greenback autograph, owns a beautiful home here, whither he has retired to enjoy the well-deserved comforts of an honored old age; and that judge Thomas Settle, of the United States Circuit Court, the original of Judge Denton in "The Fool's Errand," has another fine residence. During the winter season the great hotels (the St. James, the Windsor, the Carleton, the National, etc.) are thronged with wealthy tourists from all parts of the world, and the place has then all the gayety and animation of a leading summer resort at the North.*[12]

Travel between Jacksonville and St. Augustine became much easier with the opening of the Jacksonville, St. Augustine and Halifax River Railroad in the summer of 1883 with seven stations in between the two cities. The narrow-gauge line operated wood-burning engines and provided combination passenger and freight service. In 1885, the line was purchased by Henry Flagler, who had it widened to standard gauge. Within two years, according to a Department of the Interior report, the city of Jacksonville had become an integral part of the railroad system, serving as the eastern terminus of the Florida Central Railroad, connecting at Lake City with the Jacksonville, Pensacola and Mobile Railroad to Tallahassee and, at Baldwin, with the Atlantic, Gulf and West India Transit Railroad, for Cedar Keys to the south and Fernandina to the north. By 1875, Jacksonville was a major tourist destination and was cited by musician, poet and author Sidney Lanier, who was a frequent visitor to the city, as being "the main gateway" to Florida.

By 1887, the state of California was quickly becoming a rival for tourist dollars, so a Subtropical Exposition was held in Jacksonville to showcase Florida's horticultural, agricultural and seafood industries. Opening in January of 1888, the elaborate exposition was visited by President Grover Cleveland, and over one hundred thousand Floridians turned out to greet him.

Visitors and new residents flocked to the growing city, and the population soon rose to over one hundred thousand. But an outbreak of yellow fever that claimed the lives of over four hundred people between August and October 1888 caused the city's population to drop to approximately fourteen thousand.

The main entrance of the Southern Exposition, which was held in Jacksonville in 1887. *Courtesy of State Archives of Florida, Florida Memory, http://floridamemory.com/items/show/4633.*

Fortunately for Jacksonville and the state of Florida, Henry Morrison Flagler had become enchanted with the state during the 1880s. As the founder of what would become the Florida East Coast Railway, in 1888, he ordered the construction of a railroad bridge to cross the St. Johns River in Jacksonville. By 1892, he controlled all of the railroads in the North Florida area and was building a string of resort hotels in cities located along the railway.

By the turn of the century, Jacksonville's population had rebounded to more than twenty-eight thousand, making it the largest city in Florida. Tourists arriving by train for the winter season were plentiful, the beaches had been connected by rail lines and Henry Flagler was overseeing the construction of the Continental Hotel in Atlantic Beach.

But a devastating event took place in the late spring of 1901 that would forever change the city of Jacksonville. Just after noon on May 3, a small blaze that started at a mattress factory grew into what is still known as the Great Fire of 1901. A local reporter described the horrific scene, writing:

So fierce was the blaze and so strong the wind that millions of sparks and flying burning shingles spread over five or six blocks, setting the roofs of the houses on fire…They burned like cigar boxes, like chaff, as the thundering, mighty, lurid storm-wave of fire rolled to the east…and swept the area bare.[13]

Fire companies from as far away as Savannah fought the fire well into the night, but the city could not be saved. The path of destruction left by the fire was thirteen blocks wide and close to two miles long. In eight hours' time, the flames had destroyed 2,300 buildings, consumed 146 city blocks, left seven people dead and over ten thousand people homeless. The following morning, Mayor J.E.T. Bowden told reporters covering the story:

Say to the world, please, that the loss to Jacksonville is greater than ever before inflicted by fire upon a city of the south, but her best wealth survives in her people. I estimate our loss in property at $15,000,000. There is not a hint of lawlessness; our people of every race and condition have shown the most helpful spirit to each other and I cannot find words of commendation strong enough to express my admiration of the work done.[14]

Upon reading about the fire in the *New York Times*, "Prairie School" architect Henry John Klutho concluded all of his ongoing projects and

Jacksonville after the Great Fire of 1901. *Courtesy of State Archives of Florida, Florida Memory, http://floridamemory.com/items/show/28169.*

relocated to Jacksonville. He played a pivotal role in the reconstruction of the scorched city, where he designed numerous buildings including the St. James Building, which now serves as city hall. During the decade that followed the fire, over thirteen thousand buildings were constructed.

Although most of the downtown buildings were destroyed in the 1901 fire, the city still contains a number of historic prefire buildings in the historic districts of Riverside, Avondale, Ortega, Springfield and San Marco.

The Riverside Avondale area, which is listed in the National Register of Historic Places, is primarily a residential area, though it also contains several shopping areas, most notably Five Points and the Shoppes of Avondale. Prior to the Civil War, the area was home to several large plantations. The Magnolia Plantation, owned by Elias G. Jaudon, contained one thousand acres that produced Sea Island cotton, corn, sweet potatoes, sugar cane, cattle and sheep. He built a two-story house between 1855 and 1870, probably as a wedding gift for his son, Elias "Gabriel" Jaudon Jr., which still stands on what is now Lydia Street. The house is believed to be the oldest known building remaining in Riverside.

At the beginning of the twentieth century, Riverside Avenue was known as the "Row" and was lined with mansions. One of the remaining two houses from that time period has been carefully restored and is now operated as the Riverdale Inn.

Also located on Riverside Avenue is the Cummer Museum of Art and Gardens, which was originally the home of Ninah and Arthur Cummer in the early 1900s. The gardens, which are stunningly beautiful in the spring, contain both an English garden with a wisteria-covered arbor and an Italian garden anchored by two reflecting pools. The Cummer Gardens are listed in the National Register of Historic Places.

Ortega, in 1780, was the home of the Jones Plantation, which was occupied by Colonel Daniel McGirtt, who fought on both sides during the American Revolution but was perhaps best known for stealing cattle. Modern development of the Ortega area began in earnest with J. Pierpont Morgan's financial assistance in 1902. A wooden bridge was completed in 1908 connecting Ortega to Avondale, and the area quickly became the site of numerous mansions belonging to affluent citizens.

Although it was first established in 1869, the Springfield area north of downtown became a wealthy suburb of Jacksonville immediately after the Great Fire of 1901, when many of the city's prosperous citizens decided to build their new homes there. The historic district measures less than one square mile but contains approximately 1,800 buildings that are more than fifty years old.

The San Marco area began as a plantation built by Isaac Hendricks after he received a Spanish land grant in 1793. The only remaining plantation house in the San Marco area is the Red Bank House, originally constructed in 1857 by Albert Gallatin Philips to replace an earlier wood structure that was lost to fire. Albert was the son of a sea captain named Matthew Henry Philips, who received a Spanish land grant but had no interest in living on the property. The house, constructed of bricks molded from a clay pit located on the site, took two years to complete. The Red Bank House is a privately owned residence and is not open to visitors.

After the Civil War, the plantation properties were broken up, and the area became a farm community known as Oklahoma. Margaret Reed Mitchell, the sister of Florida governor Harrison Reed and wife of a railroad tycoon, built a winter home on a 140-acre parcel of riverfront property in 1872.

Florida's first amusement park opened in 1907 in the area then known as South Jacksonville. Dixieland Park had twenty-one acres of entertainment opportunities from which tourists could choose. There was a fine dining restaurant, a dance hall, a 1,200-seat theater, a 160-foot-high roller coaster, a toboggan ride and a hot air balloon ride. The park also housed a collection of over four hundred wild animals, including a total of eighty-seven lions, elephants and camels. Children of all ages were delighted by the merry-go-round, known as the Flying Jenny, which had fifty-six wooden animals. The park also had its own swimming pool and skating rink. Babe Ruth once played in an exhibition game at the park's baseball field, and John Phillip Sousa performed at one of the open-air concerts.

Not far from Dixieland Park, visitors could visit the Florida Ostrich Farm and the Florida Alligator Farm. Ostrich races were held daily, and available souvenirs included both feathers and eggs. At the Alligator Farm, visitors could watch alligators climb ladders and slide down chutes. They also were given the opportunity to purchase a baby alligator and have it shipped to their home, with care instructions, in a cypress box filled with Spanish moss.

Following the construction of the St. Johns River Bridge (later known as the Acosta Bridge) in 1921, the area experienced rapid growth beginning with Telfair Stockton's purchase of eighty acres of land for the development of a subdivision to be named San Marco. Carl and John Swisher, of Swisher Cigars, owned the first two homes constructed on adjoining lots in the new development.

The entrance of Dixieland Park, which was Florida's first amusement park. *Courtesy of State Archives of Florida, Florida Memory, http://floridamemory.com/items/show/34451.*

Development of the commercial area now known as San Marco Square was modeled after the Piazza San Marco in Venice and included a tiered compass-themed fountain, which was demolished in the 1990s and replaced by the new fountain containing the statues of three lions overlooking the triangular-shaped shopping district. Among the treasures to be found in the square is Theatre Jacksonville, which has been staging productions since its founding in 1919. Also known by its original name, the Little Theatre, it is one of the oldest continuously operating community theaters in the United States and has been named to the National Register of Historic Places. The nearby San Marco Theatre is an Art Deco–style single-screen movie theater that was built in 1938.

The city of South Jacksonville, which included the San Marco area, was annexed by the city of Jacksonville in 1932. Full city-county consolidation was rejected by voters at the same time, although it would be overwhelmingly approved in a 1968 referendum that allowed only the beaches and the community of Baldwin to maintain independent municipalities. At that point, the city took on the promotional nickname of "Bold New City of the South" in recognition of the city's new status as the nation's largest city in landmass.

By the early 1980s, the city's chamber of commerce was looking for a new way to promote the area and strengthen ties within the region in the hopes of securing a larger share of Florida's tourist income. The new phrase "Florida's First Coast" was selected and proved to be immensely popular among both residents and businesses. The phrase has endured and is now widely used, appropriately paying tribute to those who contributed to the history of the area as a whole.

THE KINGSLEY PLANTATION

Fort George Island, located in the northeast section of Jacksonville, is rich in both natural and historic attractions. It is the southernmost of the four sea islands of Northeast Florida, with the others being Amelia Island and the Big and Little Talbot Islands. Separated from the mainland by tidal creeks and salt marshes, this barrier island is home to an abundance of native flora and fauna.

There are two ways to access the island—from the west by taking Hecksher Drive (A1A) or from the east by taking the Mayport Ferry, which dates back to 1874, crossing the St. Johns River to Hecksher Drive, then turning onto Fort George Road. From there, it is just over half a mile to the left fork onto Palmetto Avenue, which leads to the Kingsley Plantation.

Driving through the dense forest that has reclaimed much of what were once carefully tended fields of Sea Island cotton, it is difficult to believe that over half of the island was cleared of timber when the plantation was established in 1791.

Although they are almost completely obscured by the growth of native oaks, some of the remaining sabal palms that once lined both sides of the road when it was known as the Avenue of the Palms are still visible. A visitor to Fort George Island, who arrived by "steam yacht" in 1876, mentioned the palm in the following observations of the island's landscape:

> *Your correspondent was, later in the spring, one of a party to cruise about the mouth of the St. Johns and the Sisters' Islands, and during the trip we*

landed on Fort George Island, where we were kindly driven about by the owner, who is engaged, with a number of gentlemen of taste, in forming a little Paradise. The island is not large, about eleven hundred acres. The St. Johns outlet is on the south, Fort George Inlet on the north, and the Sisters' Inlet on the west. Seaward a densely Wooded bluff, eighty feet high, shelters from the ocean gales, and beyond is a superb beach for driving, bathing, cricket, or croquet. From the bluff the view is of course very fine, and all the commerce of the St. Johns River passes near at hand. The cleared part of the island has a palmetto avenue that has no equal, and the forests are more varied than any that are accessible by drives. Shell mounds supply material for fine roads, and many drives are being laid out that are wonderfully beautiful. There is but little of the dreary formal pine; but huge bearded oaks that are worthy of druidical homage, and stately palmettos, cast deep wide shadows, while orange trees and flowering vines and shrubs fill in the scene with luxuriant bloom and foliage.[15]

Passing by the ruins of the small tabby slave homes and approaching the elegant home that lies just beyond the curve in the road, one begins to get a sense of the divergent cultures that peacefully coexisted in this very special place.

Designed in the style of a seventeenth-century gentry home and originally constructed in 1798 by the slaves of John McQueen, the house at Kingsley Plantation is believed to be the oldest existing planter's residence in the state of Florida. John McQueen wrote in a letter to his sister in 1798, "The house on the north end will be in the course of a month a very comfortable habitation, and in any other country a handsome situation."[16]

The house is built of heavy timber framing on a foundation of coquina blocks and clay bricks. The unusual floor plan, which features four one-story pavilions attached on each of the corners of the main two-story central structure, is believed to have been derived from Caribbean prototypes.

Adjacent to the main structure is a two-story kitchen house, which is thought to have been built at the same time as the main house as a single-story structure with tabby walls. An addition that included the upstairs is believed to have been constructed in the early years of the Kingsley family's ownership of the property. Other structures on the property thought to have been constructed by Kingsley include the barn and thirty-two slave cabins, of which twenty-three remain.

Zephaniah Kingsley was a maritime merchant and slave trader from South Carolina who defended the practice of slavery under the Spanish

The Kingsley Plantation House as it appeared in the 1920s. *Courtesy of State Archives of Florida, Florida Memory, http://floridamemory.com/items/show/156393.*

rules, which granted rights to slaves including the sanctity of marriage, the right to be freed for meritorious acts and the ability of slaves to purchase their own freedom with money they were allowed to earn through their own labor. He was also an activist for the legal rights of free people of color. Kingsley is quoted as having said, "Color ought not to be the badge of degradation. The only distinction should be between slave and free, not between white and colored."[17]

In the footnotes of a treatise he wrote defending the practice of slavery, he provided an insight into his own recognition of the fact that his very survival was dependent on maintaining close familial relationships with the slaves he owned by writing:

> *A patriarchal feeling of affection is due to every slave from his owner, who should consider the slave as a member of his family, whose happiness and protection is identified with that of his own family, of which his slave constitutes a part, according to his scale of condition. This affection*

creates confidence which becomes reciprocal, and is attended with the most beneficial consequences to both. It certainly is humiliating to a proud master to reflect, that he depends on his slave even for bread to eat. But such is the fact.[18]

Anna Madgigine Jai Kingsley's story is both unique and inspiring. She was captured during a slave raid by a rival tribe in West Africa when she was only thirteen years old. She was sold into slavery and shipped to Cuba, where she was purchased by Kingsley in 1806. They were married soon after, and they began their married life on a plantation named Laurel Grove, which was located in what is now the Orange Park area.

Five years after their marriage, Kingsley freed his young wife, as well as their three children, by submitting the legally binding emancipation notice to the Spanish colonial government. As a free black woman, she now was able to hold property, manage the plantations, make use of the court system and engage in business affairs.

By 1812, Anna was the owner of her own five-acre homestead with a two-story house across the river from Laurel Grove, in the area now known as Mandarin. When the fighting associated with the end of the Patriot Rebellion spread to the area during 1813, Zephaniah Kingsley was among several local planters who were captured and held in a detention camp. Anna knew that if she and her children were captured, there was every reason to believe that they would be taken north as prisoners and sold into slavery. When she learned that the Laurel Grove plantation had been plundered by the Patriots, with only the main house left unburned, she secured safe passage for herself and her children aboard a Spanish gunboat. Before the ship left the area, she took a canoe (and two men to paddle it) to the Kingsley properties on both sides of the St. Johns River and set fire to both houses to prevent them from being occupied by the Patriots. The gunboat commander praised her actions, writing, "She has worked like a heroine, destroying the strong house with the fire she set so that the artillery could not be obtained, and later doing the same with her own house."[19]

Anna herself stated to the captain that "it was more gratifying to lose it than that the enemies should take advantage."[20]

The gunboat captain, Commander Jose Antonio Moreno, made the difficult decision to abandon his pursuit of the Patriots temporarily and deliver Anna and her children to safety at the Spanish fortification at San Nicolas, where Tomas Llorente, the fort's commander, would write to the governor of her deeds, "Anna M. Kingsley deserves any favor the governor

Left: Detail of antique etched glass, which is found on the exterior doors of the Kingsley Plantation House. *Author's original image.*

Right: "Light at the Top of the Stairs," from the First Coast Reflections project, Kingsley Plantation. *Author's original image.*

can grant her. Rather than afford shelter and provisions to the enemies of His Majesty…[she] burned it all up."[21]

Zephaniah was subsequently freed. He and Anna Kingsley, along with their three children, moved to Fort George Island in 1814. Kingsley purchased the Fort George Island plantation in 1817 from its previous owner, John H. McIntosh, who had fled the Spanish by crossing the St. Mary's River into Georgia. As was the case with almost every plantation between the Georgia border and New Smyrna, the house had been looted and suffered extensive damage at the hands of the Patriots. But the house was quickly made livable, and temporary slave quarters were constructed.

Anna ran the Fort George Island plantation while her husband was away on business. She made daily checks on the health of her workers, providing care for those who were ill or injured. She and their children resided on the second story of the kitchen house, as it was customary for a married woman to live separately from her husband in her native West African homeland.

While the main crop was Sea Island cotton, they also grew citrus and sugarcane on the one thousand acres that comprised the plantation grounds at that time. Slaves at the Kingsley Plantation worked under the task system, which permitted them to engage in activities of their own choice after completion of the task assigned that day. Any proceeds earned through other activities were theirs to keep, thus providing them with the means to purchase their own freedom at half of the assessed price. Artifacts recovered during excavations conducted by National Park Service archeologists in 2010 revealed that the slaves at Kingsley Plantation were even permitted to own both muskets for hunting and pistols to be used for defense.

When Florida was ceded to the United States, the new state government began increasing restrictions against free blacks, and this eventually led to Anna's move to join her husband, who was currently in Haiti. Zephaniah Kingsley died in 1843, and Anna returned to the Jacksonville area in 1846 to live in the Arlington area home of her daughter, Mary Kingsley Sammis. The Sammis home, which was built in the 1850s, still stands and is located on Noble Circle in the Clifton subdivision. Anna lived there until her death in 1870 and is believed to be buried in the Clifton Cemetery, although no monument marks her final resting place.

Kingsley Plantation, which is listed in the National Register of Historic Places and has been designated as a Florida Heritage Landmark, is operated by the National Park Service as part of the Timucuan Ecological and Historic Preserve and hosts the Annual Kingsley Heritage Celebration each February.

In addition to the Kingsley Plantation, other historic structures on Fort George Island worthy of mention are the St. George Episcopal Church, on which construction was completed in 1884, and the Ribault Club, which began operations as a winter resort in 1928 and is now open for visitors Wednesdays through Sundays.

THE MAJOR WEBB HOUSE

Prior to European settlement, the community of Mandarin was the site of a Timucuan Indian village called Thimagua. It was the home of several large plantations while under British rule, later becoming a small farming village during the nineteenth century. The area remained predominately rural during the first half of the twentieth century. Although it has since become a large and densely populated suburb of Jacksonville, a leisurely drive down Mandarin Road, with its oak-tree canopy draped in Spanish moss, still provides a small escape from the sometimes-heavy traffic on its busy main roads.

The area now known as Mandarin was originally named Saint Anthony during the British period of Florida history. Looking to bring in new settlers, British land grants were offered to establish a plantation economy. William Bartram mentioned visiting the Greenwood plantation on the St. Johns in the vicinity of Goodby's Creek during his travels with his father, John. When William returned to Florida in 1774, he encountered a severe storm on the St. Johns River that badly damaged his small boat. He sailed his damaged boat to the "Marshall Plantation" for repairs, which was actually the Suttonia Plantation, owned by two absentee British investors, John Baker and Thomas Ashby. A resident agent named Abraham Marshall had been hired to live on the property and oversee the agricultural operations, which included the cultivation of oranges, indigo, corn and potatoes. The plantation included two large houses and separate buildings that served as the kitchen, laundry and stables. Bartram wrote of his visit with Marshall:

I spent the day in the most agreeable manner, in the society of this man of singular worth, he led me over his extensive improvements, and we returned in company with several of his neighbors. In the afternoon the most sultry time of the day, we retired to the fragrant shades of an Orange grove. The house was situated on an eminence, about one hundred and fifty yards from the river. On the right hand was the Orangery, consisting of many hundred trees, natives of the place, and left standing, when the ground about it was cleared. These trees were large, flourishing and in perfect bloom, and loaded with their ripe golden fruit.[22]

When Spain took possession of the area in 1783, it was renamed San Antonio, and for a very brief time during the Territorial period, it was known as Monroe. In 1841, the small community finally received its current name, Mandarin, when Charles Calvin Read named it after the variety of oranges he grew on his property. Driving down Brady Road today, one finds that there is an orange tree growing by the fence at the site of his former home.

During the Civil War years, Mandarin Point was the site where Confederate mines sank three Union transport ships in 1864. The sinking of these ships must have been of great comfort to the local citizens as their produce and livestock were regularly taken for the support of Union troops. For those interested in Civil War history, some of the artifacts recovered from the wreckage of the Union steamboat *Maple Leaf* are on display as part of a permanent exhibition at the Mandarin Museum.

This area also became a frequent stop for steamships looking to take on citrus fruit and vegetables for transport north during the late nineteenth century. Many who came to the area were charmed by its warm weather and quiet lifestyle.

Harriet Beecher Stowe purchased the Orange Park–area Laurel Grove plantation once owned by Zephaniah Kingsley, as a place for her son to recuperate from a head wound sustained in the Battle of Gettysburg. Stowe first visited the Mandarin area when she crossed the St. Johns River to pick up her mail in Mandarin. She and her family soon purchased a home there and visited each winter from the end of the Civil War until 1884. Although the house was demolished in 1916, several of the original decorative columns from the home's front porch are on display at the Mandarin Museum.

Stowe referred to Mandarin as a "tropical paradise" and based her book *Palmetto Leaves* on her experiences during visits to the area, including the following description of the St. Johns River:

The Mandarin-area home of Harriet Beecher Stowe, photographed in the 1870s. *Courtesy of the Library of Congress.*

The St. John's is the grand water-highway through some of the most beautiful portions of Florida; and tourists, safely seated at ease on the decks of steamers, can penetrate into the mysteries and wonders of unbroken tropical forests.[23]

She wrote of her affection for the Mandarin area in a letter to her friend Mrs. G.H. Lewes:

We have around us a little settlement of neighbors, who like ourselves have a winter home here, and live an easy, undress, picnic kind of life, far from the world and its cares.[24]

In 1872, she founded the Mandarin School, which provided education to both the African American and white children of the community. The school operated until 1929 and now serves as the home of the Mandarin Community

Club. This club also owns the old Mandarin Store and Post Office, which was built in 1911 and is located on Mandarin Road approximately one mile from the Webb House. It is open to visitors from 1:00 p.m. until 3:00 p.m. on the first and third Sundays of each month.

Mrs. Stowe and her husband, Professor Calvin E. Stowe, were instrumental in the effort to build an Episcopal church in 1880. After her husband's death in 1886, she requested that a memorial window be installed in the small church. Twenty years after her death in 1896, the Stowe Memorial window designed by Louis Comfort Tiffany was installed, featuring a peaceful scene of two Spanish moss–draped oak trees along the banks of the St. Johns River. In one panel were the names of both Harriet Beecher Stowe and her husband, Calvin, along with this excerpt from "Still, Still with Thee," a hymn whose lyrics she had written and set to Mendelssohn's "Consolation" melody:

> *In that hour, fairer than daylight dawning,*
> *Remains the glorious thought I am with Thee.*

Sadly, the church and its beautiful memorial window were completely destroyed when the community was hit by Hurricane Dora in 1964. Although the warnings had been heeded and the men of the church had covered all of the windows with plywood as the storm approached, nothing could have been done to prevent the falling of a section of a nearby tree, which destroyed the small church building.

Citrus production in the Mandarin area was the main source of income until the winter of 1894–95. On December 27, 1894, the state of Florida was hit by what is still referred to as the Great Freeze. Temperatures in the Jacksonville area fell to fourteen degrees, and the freezing temperatures persisted for two additional days. The trees were not badly damaged, as they were dormant, but the fruits that were not yet ripe enough to be harvested were all lost. Tragically, the following February brought a repeat of the record-low temperature accompanied by frost. The trees had emerged from dormancy and were especially vulnerable to the effects of the second freeze. Thousands of citrus trees throughout the state were lost. Citrus farmers reported hearing their trees "pop like pistols" as frozen sap split the bark on the tree trunks.[25] Statewide, it would take two decades for production to equal the five million boxes per year level it had obtained just prior to the freezes. The citrus industry of the Mandarin area would never recover.

The Major Webb House is located on the eastern banks of the St. Johns River, within the ten-acre Walter Jones Historical Park. Retired Union army major William Webb purchased the small house and thirty-one acres of land in 1875. In a letter to his sister Camilla, he wrote:

> *I am a full fledged Floridian now. I have secured a place on the St. Johns River in Mandarin, about ¼ mile from Mrs. Stowe's famous winter home. I shall move my family here by the 1st of Nov. and then I am buried for the next five years. I think tho' that I shall like it for I think that I have known more happiness in the past two months than has fallen to my lot for years.*[26]

Historians believe that parts of the house predate the occupancy of the Webb family, though it is believed that he added a bedroom and dining room to the original structure. It is constructed in the typical Cracker style and included a porch on three sides during the years it was home to the Webb family. Near the house is a New England saltbox–style barn that Major Webb built in 1876 from reclaimed wood from an unknown location.

On his land, Major Webb grew oranges, potatoes, cucumbers, beans and strawberries, which he sold to passing steamships from his own one thousand–foot dock, which was known as Webb's Wharf. He installed a railroad track and a single freight car that ran the full length of the dock, making the job of loading his produce aboard the steamships that stopped there much easier.

Major Webb was an active member of the Mandarin community who, like Calvin and Harriet Stowe, was involved in the negotiations that led to the construction of the Episcopal Church of Our Savior. He continued to live in the home until his death in 1893.

The house and twenty acres of land were purchased in the early 1900s by Walter Jones, an immigrant from England who owned and operated the Mandarin Store and Post Office. He enclosed the breezeway and added an additional bedroom, an indoor bathroom and a side porch.

He and his wife, Edith Mary Dawson, raised seven children during the years they lived in the house. They had a tennis court installed, and the home quickly became a favorite gathering place for friends and family.

Walter Jones died in 1928, and his daughter Agnes assumed the job of postmistress for the community of Mandarin. She and her sister Mabel Wolfe continued to live in the home into the 1990s.

The descendants of Walter Jones sold ten acres of the property and the house to the City of Jacksonville in 1993 with the understanding that it would

Above: Walter and Edith Jones at the Major Webb House, which they purchased in the 1920s. *Courtesy of the Mandarin Historical Society.*

Left: "The High Chair," from the First Coast Reflections project, Major Webb House. *Author's original image.*

serve as a historical park. Florida Communities Trust, with the addition of city and state grants, provided funding for the development and restoration of the property.

The Walter Jones Historical Park, which is located at 11964 Mandarin Road, is owned by the City of Jacksonville and has been operated as a museum since August 2000. Mandarin Museum and Historical Society has provided period furnishings in addition to some original belongings from the Jones family.

The Mandarin Historical Society provides tours of the property and house by advance reservations. They also host an annual Winter Celebration featuring musical presentations and costumed reenactors on the first Saturday of December. Park admission is free.

The Delius House

Although his father, Julius, had intended for him to assume a position in the family wool business, Frederick Delius was obviously born to create music. After being sent to various locations in his native England and in Germany, Sweden and France in failed efforts to interest him in the business, his father sent the then-twenty-two-year-old Frederick across the Atlantic Ocean to manage an orange grove on the banks of the St. Johns River.

Purchased by his father in 1884, the four-room regionalist/vernacular style house was located in an area known as Solano Grove, about forty miles south of Jacksonville and twenty miles west of St. Augustine. The plantation's property bordered the St. Johns River at a point where it is almost four miles in width, approximately halfway between the small riverfront communities of Picolata and Tocoi. Built in the style that was typical of New England homes at that time, the four-room house was originally constructed in 1882 by Guy Pride of New York.[27]

Even though the house was home to Frederick Delius for a period of only eighteen months, it was there that he wrote his first works, and the experience served as the inspiration for twelve of his later compositions. Delius would later write:

> In Florida, through sitting and gazing at nature, I gradually learnt the way in which I should eventually find myself…Hearing their singing in such romantic surroundings, it was then and there that I first felt the urge to express myself in music.

During his time at Solano Grove, Delius made frequent trips to Jacksonville, where he met Thomas Ward, the organist of a local Catholic church. The two became close friends, and Delius cited Ward's counterpoint lessons as the only lessons from which he "ever derived any benefit."[28] Delius soon hired Ward, invited him to move to Solano Grove and spent six months studying music theory under his guidance.

It was also in Florida that Frederick Delius first encountered the music of African Americans. He was inspired through a variety of sources, including the spirituals sung by waiters in the Jacksonville hotels, as well as the songs of deckhands working aboard the ships that passed by his riverfront home on their journeys between Jacksonville and Palatka.

Delius left the United States in 1886 and became the first European composer to utilize the rhythm of those songs in his compositions. Within a year of his departure, his first orchestral piece was written, and he dedicated it to the people of Florida. *The Florida Suite* contains four movements, which are entitled "Daybreak," "By the River," "Sunset Near the Plantation" and "At Night." He was, no doubt, inspired by the memories of his time at Solano Grove, as he later expressed in these words: "I used to get up

The Delius House, as it was found in the Picolata area in 1939. *Courtesy of the Jacksonville Historical Society.*

early and be spellbound watching the silent break of dawn over the river; Nature awakening—it was wonderful! At night the sunsets were all aglow—spectacular."[29] Anyone who has ever witnessed a summer sunset along the banks of the St. Johns River would not argue with his assessment of its beauty.

Even today, *The Florida Suite* is considered to be a masterpiece of orchestral music. James Arntz, creator of the 2009 PBS music special *Frederick Delius in Florida*, referred to it as "a shimmering, lushly sensuous tone poem in four exquisitely evocative movements. It portrays a time, place and atmosphere as vividly and passionately as any orchestral work in musical history."[30]

The influence of his experiences in America would surface again in the form of Walt Whitman's verses set to music in Delius's *Sea Drift*, a 1904 composition for orchestra and chorus. A new recording featuring the Florida Orchestra and the Master Chorale of Tampa Bay was made in St. Petersburg, Florida, in 2012 to celebrate the 150th anniversary of Delius's birth.

The Delius House was rediscovered in 1939 by Mrs. Martha Bullard Richmond with the recruited assistance of Mr. S.C. Middleton, the tax collector for St. Johns County; Mr. and Mrs. Edward Lawson, archivists for

"Solano Song," from the First Coast Reflections project, Delius House. *Author's original image.*

the St. Augustine Historical Society at the time; and a taxi driver named Iles Colee, who had been turkey hunting in the area with Mr. Middleton. Traveling more than six miles of unpaved roads by taxi, they finally located the small house hidden under years of underbrush growth. Mrs. Richmond purchased the Delius House and two acres of property in 1943 and donated both to Jacksonville University.[31] The Delius House was moved to the school's University Boulevard campus in 1961. It has been restored with the assistance of contributions by the Delius Trust in London and other donors. Inside the home are two period pianos as well as other period furnishings, Delius Festival memorabilia and photos of Frederick Delius. It is open for tours by appointment only.

THE MERRILL HOUSE

The son of a blacksmith, James E. Merrill cofounded Merrill-Stevens Engineering in partnership with his brother, James Eugene, and Alonzo Stevens in 1887. The Merrill-Stevens firm would become one of the largest shipbuilding companies in the South and, by 1906, was home to the largest dry dock between New Orleans and Newport News. By 1918, they had a floating dock capable of lifting over 4,000 tons, a marine railway and three electric hoists, one of which could lift over 250 tons.

Vessels built at the shipyards included barges used in the construction of the Panama Canal, many of the steamships that operated on the St. Johns River and ships that were used in both world wars, including twenty-eight Liberty ships. The assembly line methods used in the mass production of Liberty ships resulted in technological advances, including the cold rolling of steel and innovative welding techniques that produced the first all-welded ships. These advances made it possible to build ships in an average of forty-two days, providing the Allied forces the ability to quickly replace cargo ships that were sunk by German U-boats.

Merrill originally built this two-story Queen Anne–style home in 1886 on Lafayette Street, not far from the shipyard. The house was moved, and the original address is no longer in existence, as it is now the site of the Jacksonville Veterans Memorial Arena. The house, with its square tower and decorative gables and shingles, also features Eastlake-style posts, brackets and spindles on the front porch.

The Merrill House; date of photograph unknown. *Courtesy of the Jacksonville Historical Society.*

The Merrill House contains twelve rooms decorated with period furnishings that were collected over a two-year period by the Jacksonville Historical Society. Most of the items were donated by Jacksonville citizens, including a painting by portrait and landscape artist Julia Dupre Bounetheau, who had studied art in Paris in 1856. She and her husband, fellow artist Henry Brintnell Bounetheau, both taught art at the Madame Julia Dupre's Seminary, the largest and most select school for young ladies in Charleston, South Carolina. The Smithsonian American Art Museum has a portrait of her, which was painted in watercolor on ivory by her husband, in their collection.

An antique hall tree in the entrance of the Merrill House. *Author's original image.*

One of Bounetheau's paintings that hangs in the Merrill House has two small burn holes in its surface. Julia Dupre Bounetheau's son, Henry, lost his life retrieving items, including his mother's painting, from his home during the Great Fire of 1901. He was quoted as having said, "I cannot leave my mother's picture; it is the only one we have."[32]

The Merrill House was scheduled for demolition in 1999, but the Jacksonville Historical Society acquired the structure in the year 2000 and undertook the five-year-long restoration project to save the home. The structure had to be moved twice during restoration to ensure it was not damaged during the construction of the nearby Baseball Grounds of Jacksonville.

The Merrill House is now located at 319 A. Philip Randolph Boulevard and is maintained as a museum by the Jacksonville Historical Society, which also owns and operates the circa 1887 Old St. Andrews Episcopal Church located next door to the Merrill House. St. Andrews is the largest church to survive the Great Fire of 1901. Tours of the Merrill House are available by appointment.

JACKSONVILLE BEACHES AREA

The beaches just east of Jacksonville were settled in the 1830s when river pilots and fishermen began making their homes in the Mayport area. In addition to the fishing industry, the area also had a growing lumber industry and was known as Mayport Mills until after the Civil War. The lighthouse, which now stands within the boundaries of the Mayport Naval Station, was erected in 1858 to replace two previous lighthouses that were lost to erosion. The population of Mayport by 1885 totaled approximately six hundred, and the small town had its own post office and school. Steamships from Jacksonville made daily stops, bringing visitors to the beach.

In 1886, the Jacksonville, Mayport, Pablo Railway and Navigation Company was established by Alexander Wallace, a Scottish immigrant who had served in the Union naval blockade during the Civil War. He was also the owner of the Alligator Lumber Mill in Jacksonville and a director of the National Bank of the State of Florida. By the time of his death in 1889, the JMP Railway had gone bankrupt and was subsequently purchased by Henry Flagler.

Further south along the coast, the area now known as Jacksonville Beach was just beginning to see development. In 1883, it was known as the community of Ruby, though it would be renamed Pablo Beach just three years later. Development of the area began in earnest with the establishment of the Jacksonville and Atlantic Railway Company and the construction of seventeen miles of light-gauge track running from South Jacksonville to the Murray Hall Hotel in Pablo Beach.

The Murray Hall was built by a wealthy Jacksonville merchant named John G. Christopher and was located at the current intersection of Beach Boulevard and First Street North. It was an elaborate three-story structure with turrets and porches, a water supply provided by artesian wells and electricity from its own power plant. It was advertised as the "finest and most elegantly furnished hotel in the South," and its 192 guest rooms provided luxurious accommodations for up to 350 guests.

The hotel, as well as the train station and some additional surrounding structures, was lost to a fire in August 1890. A total of five other resort hotels were constructed in the following years, but these were eventually lost to fires as well.

By 1889, the Jacksonville and Atlantic Railway Company was in financial trouble and was purchased by Henry Flagler. He changed the light-gauge lines out for standard gauge with sixty-pound rails, extended the line to Mayport and incorporated the small railway into his Florida East Coast Railway. The first FEC train arrived in Pablo Beach on March 9, 1900.

Pablo Beach was incorporated in 1909 and saw the construction of its first five-block-long boardwalk in 1915. Owned by the Pablo Development and Power Company, the boardwalk known as Little Coney Island was

The Murray Hall in Pablo Beach (now Jacksonville Beach) in 1888. *Courtesy of State Archives of Florida, Florida Memory, http://floridamemory.com/items/show/145764.*

constructed entirely of wood and featured concession stands, a dance hall, a billiards room and a roller skating rink. But the wooden structure was continually battered by storms, and it was condemned in 1924. A replacement boardwalk was built in 1927 but was destroyed by fire in 1933.

A new source of entertainment arrived with the increasing popularity of automobiles, whose owners began using the beaches' hard-packed sand for racing. Joe Lander broke the stock car speed record on the Atlantic-Pablo Beaches Course in 1906 by driving five miles in less than five minutes. In March 1911, two speed records were broken on the same day at the course when Bob Burman drove his Buick "Bug" at just above ninety miles per hour in the twenty-mile-long "free-for-all" race, and Howard Wilcox set a new one-mile record of 40.32 seconds in his National stock car. The Atlantic-Pablo Beaches Course races continued until the United States entered World War I in 1917.

Although the boardwalks and auto races brought many visitors to the area, the main source of entertainment at the beaches was the opportunity to play in the water, though the surf proved to be dangerous on occasion. The United States Volunteer Life Savings Corps was formed in 1912 following the drowning of a young nurse named Mary E. Proctor. The town of Pablo Beach provided a building for the corps in 1913. The original building has been replaced several times, but the Life Guard Station has continually occupied the same oceanfront lot, where Beach Boulevard meets the Atlantic Ocean. Today, the volunteer lifeguard tradition continues, with more than 120 active members serving the community of Jacksonville Beach.

The first pier was constructed in 1922 by Charles Shad, a tailor and men's clothier from Jacksonville. It was twenty-five feet wide, four hundred feet long and was equipped with electric lights that made it visible for several miles up and down the coastline. At the end of the pier was a large dance hall that hosted a marathon dance with $1,000 of prize money in 1923. The original pier was lost to a fire in 1937.

The bond issue for the first lighted concrete highway connecting the beach to Jacksonville was passed by the county government in 1923. Ties between the beaches and the city were further strengthened when Pablo Beach was renamed Jacksonville Beach in 1925.

The Naval Section Base at Mayport was commissioned in December 1942 and first served as the homeport for minesweepers and a fueling station for submarines. Although the base was decommissioned at the end of World War II, it was reactivated in 1948 and expanded to provide runways for navy aircraft. By 1952, aircraft carriers were making use of the basin, which had been dredged to a depth of forty-two feet. Today, the Naval Station Mayport covers more than 3,400 acres and is the third-largest naval facility in the continental United States.

The beaches area east of Jacksonville now includes the cities of Mayport, Atlantic Beach, Neptune Beach and Jacksonville Beach. Combined, they offer twenty-two miles of white sand beaches and Kathryn Abbey Hanna Park, an all-too-rare unsoiled area of coastal hammock totaling over four hundred acres.

THE FOREMAN'S HOUSE

Once, Jacksonville residents and visitors could enjoy a day at Pablo Beach by taking a fifteen-mile ride aboard the Florida East Coast Railway. Pablo Beach, which later became Jacksonville Beach, was described in FEC literature as a "small village, pleasantly and conveniently located midway between Jacksonville and St. Augustine. More free from mosquitoes and other insects than any other location in the State."[33]

Railroad travel to the beach had ended by 1933, although rail travel aboard the Florida East Coast Railway throughout the state continued until the final run on July 30, 1968. Beach Boulevard was constructed on the right of way belonging to the former Florida East Coast Railway's Jacksonville to Pablo Beach line, and was opened to automobile traffic in the late 1930s.

Located in the Pablo Historical Park at Jacksonville Beach, the Foreman's House was built by the Florida East Coast Railway Company in 1900 and was originally located one block from where it currently stands. It is number ninety-three of literally hundreds of foreman's houses built between Northeast Florida and Key West, all using the same floor plan and painted the same "colonial yellow" color. Each of these small one-and-a-half-story houses contained a kitchen, living room, dining room, two bedrooms and an attic space.

Although it is not known who first occupied this particular house, it is known that a section foreman named Hershel Smith lived in the house from 1915 until 1922 with his wife, Ethel, and their two daughters. The house had no electricity and no indoor plumbing at the time, and the kitchen

A vintage image of the Foreman's House. Note the railroad tracks, which were located on what is now Beach Boulevard. Date unknown. *Courtesy of Beaches Area Historical Society.*

was equipped with a wood-burning stove. The floors were constructed of tongue-and-groove cypress, and the roof was covered in cypress shingles. An engineering report dated 1916 placed a value of $997 on the house.

The Foreman's House was donated to the Beaches Area Historical Society in 1979 by William T. Brown, who had purchased the house for sixty dollars in 1933, and it became the cornerstone of the Pablo Historical Park. The Beaches Area Historical Society oversaw the restoration of the structure and filled it with carefully selected furnishings appropriate to the time period of its construction.

In a letter written to the historical society, Jim Garner, a former Seaboard Air Line Railroad employee, wrote about his childhood memories of visiting the house when it was occupied by an unnamed family with six children— three boys and three girls. He spoke fondly of the attic as "a haven for the boys, playing, talking, building boats" and of a "piano for the girls" in the small living room. He also remembered "picking and singing on Sunday afternoons with guitars, banjos and fiddles, the family and brother of the missus of the house, plenty of love, warmth, laughter, family closeness."[34]

The Foreman's House is one of four historic buildings on the grounds of the Pablo Historical Park. The other buildings include the Beaches Museum Chapel, which was originally built as one of the Episcopal "river churches" in 1887; the train depot, which was built in 1900 (at the same time as the Foreman's House); and the 1903 Pablo Beach Post Office. The park is also home to a twenty-five-ton steam locomotive built in 1911, which was donated to the Beaches Area Historical Society by the City of St. Augustine in 1981 and is now housed in a glass enclosure that faces Beach Boulevard.

The Pablo Historical Park, which has been designated as a Florida Heritage Landmark, is located at 381 Beach Boulevard in Jacksonville Beach. Museum hours are Tuesday through Saturday from 10:00 a.m. until 4:00 p.m. and Sunday from noon until 4:00 p.m. Tours are available on the hour beginning at 11:00 and ending at 3:00.

ST. AUGUSTINE

The city of St. Augustine is located thirty-five miles south of Jacksonville. The historic heart of the city lies between two saltwater rivers, the San Sebastian River to the west and the Matanzas River to the east, and is separated from the Atlantic Ocean by Anastasia Island.

St. Augustine is widely recognized as the oldest continuously occupied European-established settlement in the continental United States. It was founded by the Spanish in September 1565, but was ceded by treaties several times prior to the United States' control of the territory of Florida that began in 1819.

The story of early Spanish efforts to explore and settle Florida is one of great courage and sacrifice. Juan Ponce de Leon, the first documented European to land in Florida, arrived near St. Augustine in the year 1513. He died just eight years later from wounds received in an attack by the Calusa Indians in the Charlotte Harbor area of Southwest Florida.

Palfina de Narváez landed near Tampa Bay in 1528 with more than six hundred men and, after exploring the interior, ordered the construction of rafts to return to the sea via an inland river. His raft was pulled out to sea by a storm, and he was never seen again. Only four of his men survived, arriving in Mexico City on foot eight years later.

Hernando de Soto landed in the Tampa Bay area in 1539. He led eight hundred men on a four-year-long expedition that covered eleven present-day states and ventured as far west as the mouth of the Mississippi River. It was there he fell ill and died.

An aerial view of the historic district in the heart of St. Augustine, including the campus of Flagler College, the Lightner Museum and the restored Casa Monica Hotel. *Author's original image.*

When compared to the successful exploits of Hernando Cortez in Mexico and Francisco Pizarro in Peru, any further expenditure in Florida seemed to be a poor investment. Yet in spite of the previous heavy losses, King Phillip II of Spain was determined to gain control of Florida, and the founding of Fort Caroline by the French prompted a renewed effort that would ultimately prove to be successful.

The founding of the city of St. Augustine took place on September 8, 1565, when Pedro Menéndez de Avilés came ashore after a long and difficult voyage. He had departed the southern port of Cadiz, Spain, in June 1565 with a fleet of eleven ships carrying over two thousand sailors, soldiers and their families and a handful of priests. By the time he arrived in Florida on September 7, his fleet had only five remaining ships, and the number of settlers had been reduced to approximately eight hundred. Along the way, they had encountered storms that were so fierce that Father Francisco López de Mendoza Grajales wrote:

> *Very often the sea washed completely over the deck where we were gathered, one hundred and twenty men having no other place to go, as there was only*

one between-decks, and that was full of biscuit, wine, and other provisions. We were in such great danger that it was found necessary to lighten the vessel, and we threw a great many barrels of water into the sea, as well as our cooking apparatus and seven millstones which we were taking with us. Most of the reserve rigging and the great ship's cable were cast overboard, and still the waves continued to break over us. The admiral then resolved to throw all the chests of the men into the sea, but the distress of the soldiers was so great that I felt constrained to throw myself at his feet and beg him not to do it. I reminded him that we ought to trust to the great mercy of our Lord, and, like a true Christian, he showed confidence in God, and spared the luggage. When Jesus Christ permitted the return of day, we looked at each other as at men raised from the dead.[35]

Given their struggles at sea, it is not surprising that Father Mendoza Grajales was the first to come ashore carrying a cross to signal the successful end of their journey and the beginning of their mission. When Menéndez came ashore with his contingent of six hundred settlers, he did so with banners flying and trumpet sounding, but humbly knelt to kiss the cross.

Don Pedro Menéndez de Avilés was sent to Florida under orders from his king to remove the French settlers from Fort Caroline. Having learned of the Spanish plans, the majority of the French contingent boarded ships and set sail for St. Augustine to challenge the Spanish there. At the same time, the Spanish were already marching north toward Fort Caroline, the location of which had been revealed to them by a mutinous French soldier they had captured.

The Spanish marched for three days over difficult swampy terrain, arriving on the evening of September 19. When they launched their attack the following morning, they found the garrison to be so poorly defended that the battle to take the fort lasted less than an hour. Not a single Spanish soldier was lost in the battle.

Meanwhile, the French who had departed for St. Augustine sailed directly into the path of a hurricane, which quickly claimed their ships and left approximately two hundred survivors stranded on the southern shores of what is now known as Matanzas Inlet. The ill-fated French attempt to attack the Spanish on their own ground eventually led, not once but twice, to the surrender and execution of all but a handful of the shipwreck survivors. The first group to be captured and killed on September 29 included just over 110 French soldiers. Their location was revealed to Menéndez by natives who were friendly with the Spanish. Menéndez marched 50 of his soldiers south to the inlet and informed the stranded French of his capture of Fort Caroline. Having no other option available, they surrendered and were executed somewhere in the sand dunes north of the inlet. A second group of shipwrecked survivors, which included Jean Ribault and over 130 men under his command, was also captured and executed approximately two weeks later on October 12. Only those who professed to be of the Catholic faith were spared.

The tragic outcome of those encounters, while unthinkable under the rules of modern warfare, can be viewed differently when all circumstances of the moment are considered. In both cases, the forces of Menéndez were outnumbered, so there would have been considerable risk involved in capturing such a large number of prisoners so far from the Spanish encampment. Further, food and shelter were in very short supply, and with winter approaching, the likelihood of starvation among settlers would have increased exponentially with the addition of several hundred prisoners. Finally, he was under orders from his king to remove the threat of French encroachment as well as that of Protestant heresy. Yet, even taking all of these factors into consideration, the executions still remain as one of the most tragic events of the area's history.

The sad events at Matanzas Inlet finally secured complete Spanish control of the area that would last for more than two hundred years.

The city of St. Augustine began to take shape during the First Spanish Period with the construction of the Castillo de San Marcos, the Mission Nombre de Dios and the simple structures that served as homes to the early settlers.

The first homes were built with the assistance of the local natives and were constructed of wooden post frames; walls of woven branches, canes or reed; and plastered over with clay. Roof structures were made of pine rafters and palm thatch. The chief carpenter who was assigned to the Menéndez voyage, Martin de Yztuera, is considered by researchers to be the person most likely responsible for the style of board construction utilized in building the homes of middle-class settlers in St. Augustine.

All of those simply constructed homes would be lost to fire within eight months, during an attack on the settlement by the Saturiwa natives. The destruction was documented by Bartolome Barrientos, who wrote:

Fire arrows were showered on the houses at night whenever a breeze was blowing. The sparks caught and nothing could stop them. The powder ignited and flames engulfed cloth, linen, stores, and the flags and standards, both those belonging to the Adelantado and those won by him from the Lutherans. So thoroughgoing was the Indian incendiarism that nothing could be salvaged.[36]

Although the town was quickly rebuilt, St. Augustine was to suffer destruction again in late May 1586 when Sir Francis Drake led a fleet of twenty-three ships and two thousand soldiers on a raid that was ordered by England's Queen Elizabeth I.

Ironically, it was this event that led to the first map of St. Augustine, which was created by Giovanni Baptista Boazio, an Italian draftsman and cartographer who worked in London. Boazio served as the mapmaker for Drake's voyage to the West Indies and Spanish Florida. The engraved, hand-colored map of St. Augustine is the oldest item in the State Archives of Florida and is also believed to be the earliest printed plan of any American city. It showed a typical plan for Spanish colonies of rectangular blocks containing rectangular lots. There were eleven blocks depicted in the small settlement, which was home to approximately four hundred Spanish colonists at the time. Those same blocks are still in existence today.

A detail from a 1586 Boazio map showing the original eleven blocks of St. Augustine and the fort. *Courtesy of the Library of Congress.*

Boazio's map also illustrated the attacks on both the city and the fort, which his notes described as having been constructed of "the bodies of Cedar trees" and containing "some fourteen great and long pieces of artillery."

Drake's men forced the Spanish to retreat into the surrounding wilderness, captured both the fort and the town and burned both to the ground before departing for the English settlement of Roanoke Island two days later.

Menéndez and the Spanish settlers returned to what was left of their settlement and solicited financial aid from the viceroy of Cuba to rebuild. But the town was attacked and plundered again by Robert Searle, an English privateer, in 1668 as an act of revenge for a Spanish attack on the English settlement of New Province in the Bahamas. It was this attack on St. Augustine that led to the commitment by Queen Regent Mariana, the widow of King Philip IV, to have a masonry fort built to defend the city. This marked the beginning of construction with coquina, which was locally mined in St. Augustine.

Coquina is a naturally forming sedimentary rock, comprised mainly of shell, which was found by the Spanish on Anastasia Island in 1580. The quarries located within the Anastasia State Recreation Area are open to visitors, although the site is a protected historic area and nothing can be removed. Natural coquina outcroppings can be found on the beach at Washington Oaks Gardens State Park, located on Highway A1A approximately twenty miles south of St. Augustine.

Construction of the Castillo de San Marcos began in 1672. It is the oldest masonry fort in the United States and an outstanding example of the bastion style of fortification, a style that evolved as a result of the military use of gunpowder and explosive shells. The fort is constructed almost entirely of coquina mined on Anastasia Island by the Spanish settlers and the Timucua natives, transported over land by ox-drawn carts to the shore and then ferried across Matanzas Bay on wooden rafts. Labor for the construction of the fort was provided by Native Americans from the Guale, Timucua and Apalache nations as well as skilled Cuban laborers working under the supervision of the Spanish settlers.

The construction was plagued by problems such as insufficient funding, late arrival of supply ships, attacks by pirates, battles with the British and illness among those overseeing the project. The chief engineer, Ignacio Daza, died after only seven months in Florida. In spite of the numerous setbacks, which once delayed all work for a period of two years, the fort was finally completed in 1695.

Coquina outcroppings at Washington Oaks Beach, south of St. Augustine. The use of coquina as a building material began in colonial St. Augustine. *Author's original image.*

The use of local coquina for construction proved to be a very fortunate choice, as the fort withstood the repeated cannon fire of the British forces led by James Oglethorpe, founder of the colony of Georgia, when they attacked the city in 1740. Oglethorpe's men set up their cannons on Anastasia Island across from the Castillo de San Marcos. The British bombardment of the fort lasted for twenty-seven days. Unlike other materials, the soft and porous nature of the coquina enabled it to absorb the repeated strong impacts of cannon fire without shattering. Oglethorpe abandoned his efforts to take the city when a fierce storm approached, forcing him to set sail so quickly that he left his own artillery behind.

The use of coquina as a building material can also be found in the remaining homes that were constructed during this period. The first floors of the González-Alvarez, Father O'Reilly, Tovar and Fernandez-Llambias houses are all built of coquina. In one exterior wall of the Tovar house, a cannonball believed to be from Oglethorpe's 1740 attack remains embedded in the coquina.

The homes built during this period were typical of Spanish colonial architectural style. They were simple single-story structures with flat roofs, shuttered windows with no glass and loggias opening onto the yards through an arcade with arches.

The unsuccessful 1740 attack by British forces under the command of James Oglethorpe prompted the construction of the nearby Fort Matanzas, to guard against ships sailing upriver to attack the Castillo. When Oglethorpe arrived again in 1792 with a fleet of twelve ships, he sent a scouting expedition in small boats into the inlet. The Spanish soldiers fired a single shot from the fort's cannons. The small boats returned to the British ships, all of which quickly departed. This was the only hostile shot ever fired from Fort Matanzas.

The British finally gained control of Florida and the city of St. Augustine in 1763 as part of an exchange involving the return of Havana to the Spanish at the end of the Seven Years' War. However, they would only hold the territory for slightly more than twenty years.

With the start of the American Revolution came an influx of new settlers to the still–British held area of Florida. The population of St. Augustine grew quickly, and the new British inhabitants left their mark on the city in the form of changes to the existing Spanish colonial style homes. Second stories with covered balconies were added, glass was placed in windows and entries were moved from the walled gardens to the fronts of homes so they opened onto the street.

British control came to an end via the Treaty of Paris, and by the summer of 1784, the Second Spanish Period began with the return of the Castillo to Spanish governor Vicente Manuel de Cespedes.

This period began with the departure of the British inhabitants for colonies in the Caribbean, and the new Spanish governor offering land grants, ten-year tax-free occupancy and cash bonuses to attract new settlers. In 1786, the restriction against non-Catholic settlers was also dropped, and the Spanish government began to allow slave holders for the first time.

But by 1800, the once-powerful empire of Spain had lost much of its economic power, and Florida had become less Spanish due to the arrival of settlers from the newly formed United States. Attacks by these new settlers on the towns of Native Americans and the resulting reprisal attacks by Native Americans in neighboring Georgia caused the United States Army to lead frequent incursions into the Spanish territory of Florida. By the end of the Second Seminole War in 1818, Spanish control of East Florida had been lost, and the February 22, 1819 signing of the Adams-Onis Treaty formally ceded control of Florida to the United States.

It was during the Territorial Period, which lasted from 1821 until 1845, that John James Audubon came to St. Augustine to collect specimens for his Birds of America book series. The Castillo de San Marcos can be seen in the background of his painting of the Greenshank. He referred to the city as resembling "an old French village…with streets about 10 feet wide and deeply sanded."[37] Arriving in late November and working in the area during the winter of 1831–32, Audubon discovered and documented fifty-two types of birds that were previously unknown to him. But he returned to Charleston as the winter came to an end, having grown weary of being plagued by the mosquitoes and "surrounded by thousands of Alligators."[38]

Ralph Waldo Emerson arrived in the city in the winter of 1827, seeking a warmer climate to ease the symptoms of his tuberculosis. In his poem "St. Augustine," Emerson wrote of his arrival:

> *Full swelled the sail before the driving wind,*
> *Till the stout pilot turned his prow to land,*
> *Where peered, mid orange groves & citron boughs,*
> *The little city of Saint Augustine.*
>
> *Slow slid the vessel to the fragrant shore,*
> *Loitering along Matanzas' sunny waves,*
> *And under Anastasia's verdant isle.*
> *I saw Saint Mark's grim bastions, piles of stone*
> *Planting their deep foundations in the sea,*
> *And speaking to the eye a thousand things*
> *Of Spain, a thousand heavy histories.*
> *Under these bleached walls of old renown*
> *Our ship was moored.*
> *—An hour of busy noise,*
> *And I was made a quiet citizen,*
> *Pacing my chamber in a Spanish street*

Further on in the poem, he pays tribute to the history of the area with these lines:

> *Yet much is here*
> *Than can beguile the months of banishment*
> *To the pale travellers whom Disease hath sent*
> *Hither for genial air from Northern homes.*

Oh many a tragic story can be read,—
Dim vestiges of a romantic past,
Within the small peninsula of sand.
Here is the old land of America
And in this sea-girt nook, the infant steps
First foot-prints of that Genius giant-grown
That daunts the nations with his power today. [39]

While the city might have held limited appeal for Audubon, and Emerson may have found some aspects of it to be grim, others found St. Augustine to be delightful. A young army lieutenant who visited St. Augustine several times in 1842 found the city's social life to be highly entertaining, writing:

Balls, masquerades, etc. are celebrated during the gay season of the Carnival. Indeed, I have never seen anything like it—dancing, dancing and nothing but dancing, but not such as you see in the north. Such ease and grace I have never before beheld. A lady will waltz all evening without fatigue, because it is done slowly, with grace. [40]

That remembrance was written by William Tecumseh Sherman, who would later be promoted to the position of general in the Union army during the Civil War and would employ a devastating "scorched earth" policy during his March to the Sea campaign through the state of Georgia.

Henry Flagler arrived in the 1880s and began turning St. Augustine into a winter resort for well-heeled visitors. He bought and incorporated local railroads to create the Florida East Coast Railway and headquartered his business in the city. He then commissioned the construction of a number of large and elegant buildings including the Spanish Renaissance Revival–style Ponce de Leon Hotel, which now serves as the campus of Flagler College. He was instrumental in the construction of a number of churches and the city's first hospital. He also played a part in the construction of a baseball field that was home to one of the first Negro League teams. His vision of converting St. Augustine into the "Newport of the South" would have lasting effects that are still evident today, not only in St. Augustine but throughout many of the eastern coastal cities of Florida.

In 1895, the first bridge to Anastasia Island was built. It was constructed entirely of wood and required almost constant maintenance and repairs. Calls for replacement of the bridge were frequent by the 1920s, and Henry Rodenbaugh, the vice president and bridge expert for Henry Flagler's Florida

St. Augustine's beautiful and historic Bridge of Lions, photographed in 1936. *Courtesy of the Library of Congress.*

East Coast Railway, organized a bond issue to finance the new bridge. The new bridge would become more than a way to cross the Matanzas Bay. It would become a landmark.

The Bridge of Lions is one of the city's most iconic and beautiful structures. Completed in 1927, the cost of the bridge was approximately ten times more expensive than simple utilitarian bridges of the same size. However, the bridge was intended to be a landmark. The structure, designed by the J.E. Greiner Company of Baltimore, incorporated Mediterranean Revival elements to complement the city's Spanish origins and architecture. In the center of the span, four lighted Spanish Colonial–inspired octagonal towers provided a focal point, and period luminaires graced both sides of the span from bank to bank. The western entrance to the bridge was to be guarded by a pair of marble Medici-style lions, which were commissioned by Dr. Andrew Anderson II and carved by F. Romanelli of Florence.

Over the years, "improvements" were made to the bridge, though clearly not enough attention was paid to historic details in some cases. In 1971, the original ornate railings and luminaires were removed and replaced with modern tubular railings and lighting units.

Due to cracks found in the support structure, the bridge was closed in 2006, and the debate between those who wanted to restore the bridge and those who wanted to replace it began. But after the National Trust for Historic Preservation named the Bridge of Lions as one of "America's 11 Most Endangered Historic Places," a team of engineers, designers, landscapers, architects and historians was assembled to work with preservationists on a restoration project. An innovative interior steel framework and new foundation system hidden within the existing structure was designed and installed. The original design plans were used to recreate the ornate railing. Additionally, the original specifications for the luminaires had been preserved and kept at the St. Augustine Historical Society, making it possible to replicate the original lighting, which had been removed and replaced with aluminum pole lighting in the 1970s.

The newly restored Bridge of Lions, which opened in early 2010, still features the four towers and twenty-three pairs of graceful arches. The new double-lantern light posts were installed, and the bridge was repainted to match the original gray-green color uncovered by researchers. Even the much-loved lions underwent restoration work and returned in March 2011 to continue serving as sentinels of the much-beloved bridge.

The story of the restoration work that saved the Bridge of Lions is testament to the dedication of St. Augustine's current leaders and citizens to maintain and enhance the historic character of their city.

St. Augustine today contains a large historic district known as Old Town. The heart of the city is its downtown Plaza de la Consitucion, with the majority of its most historic buildings located within several blocks both to the north and to the south of the plaza. The Old Town district was recognized as a United States National Historic Landmark District in 1970 and contains a total of 220 historic buildings located within a twenty-two-block area. The boundaries of the district are based on the old walled city as established by the Spanish and British during the colonial development that took place between 1656 and 1821.

Many of the buildings that now house the retail shops and restaurants on both sides of St. George Street north of the plaza are reconstructions dating from the 1960s. It is important to note that the reconstruction of these buildings, most of which disappeared during the British period, was based on historical research and archeological evidence. In most cases, the structures were rebuilt on their original eighteenth-century foundations.

One of two Medici lions at the western entrance of the newly restored Bridge of Lions.
Author's original image.

Fortunately, there are a number of remaining original buildings scattered throughout the historic district that have been carefully preserved and restored.

Additional historic districts within the city of St. Augustine include the Abbott Tract, the Model Land Company area and Lincolnville. The Abbott Tract, located east of San Marco Avenue between Pine Street and the Castillo de San Marcos, contains the largest concentration of nineteenth-century homes in the city. The Model Land Company area, located east of Ponce de Leon Boulevard between Orange and Cordova Streets, contains numerous historic structures that were built near the end of the "Flagler Era" of the city's development. Lincolnville consists of a forty-five-block area west of Maria Sanchez Lake between Cedar and Cerro Streets and was founded in 1866 by former slaves.

The city also contains many beautiful historic churches that are open to visitors, including the Memorial Presbyterian Church, which was built by Henry Flagler in 1889. The Venetian Renaissance–style church was dedicated in honor of his only daughter, Jennie Louise Benedict, who died of complications following the birth of her own daughter, who also died just hours after her birth.

Visitors who are seeking more than day tours of historic homes will be happy to know that guest accommodations are available in a number of bed-and-breakfast inns located in historic structures. The beautifully restored Moorish Revival–style Casa Monica Hotel offers a variety of accommodations from standard rooms to a four-story, three-bedroom suite for those seeking a taste of Flagler-era elegance during their visit to St. Augustine.

In addition to the homes described in the following sections of this book, visitors to St. Augustine with a strong interest in the military history of the area would be well advised to visit the Castillo de San Marcos and Fort Matanzas. Those interested in the Gilded Age development of the city should visit the Spanish Renaissance–style campus of Flagler College, which was originally built as the Ponce de Leon Hotel. Especially noteworthy items among the many opulent features are the seventy-nine Louis Comfort Tiffany stained glass windows in the dining room and the Tiffany Austrian crystal chandeliers located in the Flagler Room.

There are three basic floor plans that were used in early St. Augustine home construction. In the late 1700s, the vast majority of homes were based on the Common Plan, which featured a single- or one-and-a-half-story structure, with one large room or two smaller rooms, and a sleeping loft. The main entrance of a Common Plan house sometimes opened onto the street. The kitchen of this style of home was typically detached, as is the case with the González-Alvarez House. The second style of home, referred to as the St. Augustine Plan, may be either one or two stories. They commonly contain two or four larger rooms and have either a loggia or sheltered porch. A two-story St. Augustine Plan home would likely have a balcony overlooking the street, but the main entrance would be located in the loggia and would open onto the yard. The Fernandez-Llambias House is a good example of this style of structure. The third style of home, which was much less commonly utilized, is the Wing Plan and is easily recognized by the L- or U-shaped footprint of the structure. These larger and more elaborate buildings were usually home to government officials or prominent families. The entry door usually opened onto the yard or patio. The Ximenez-Fatio House perfectly illustrates this plan, especially since it has undergone very few structural changes since its initial construction.

One can also tell a great deal about the origin of construction in St. Augustine by the choice of building materials that were used. Much of the early Spanish wall construction utilized either tabby, a simple type of lime-based mortar used in modest homes, or coquina block, which was more commonly used in the construction of better homes. Window openings contained no glass and were instead covered with *rejas*, which are a type of projecting exterior grating constructed of wood strips and used on ground-level windows, and were often accompanied by interior shutters. Homes built during the British Period, and modifications made to existing homes at that time, made use of wood as the primary material for the construction of walls. Double-hung window sashes were typically nine-over-six panes on the ground floors and six-over-six on the second floors. British-built houses featured wood exterior shutters that were solid on ground floors and louvered on upper floors. It is not uncommon to find homes with a combination of both Spanish and British construction, with ground-level walls of coquina and second-story walls built of wood.

One thing that is common to all St. Augustine homes is that each has a unique character that is always accompanied by a certain level of charm. There is a sense of Old World elegance to be found in even the most simple of homes. More importantly, the respectful restoration work that has been done on these homes is most admirable. That fact alone stands as clear evidence that the people of St. Augustine truly understand the value of their historic treasures.

THE GONZÁLEZ-ALVAREZ HOUSE

B uilt sometime after the British burning of the city of St. Augustine in 1702, this coquina house originally contained only two rooms. Tomás González y Hernández, a twenty-year-old Spanish sailor from Tenerife who became an artilleryman at the Castillo de San Marcos, was the first recorded occupant of the original single-story coquina structure located at 14 St. Francis Street. He married Francisca Guevara y Dominguez, whose family had been in St. Augustine for four generations, and their residency in the house was noted in the 1727 burial record of their unnamed son. The house was also shown on the de la Puente map of 1763 and was listed as the property of Hernández. He, his wife and their six surviving children lived in the house for over forty years, until they were forced to leave when Spanish Florida was ceded to Great Britain in 1763 in exchange for the return of Cuba.

A British soldier and paymaster for England's east coast troops, Sergeant Major Joseph Peavett, purchased the home in 1775 and doubled its size by adding the wood-frame second story, a balcony and a fireplace. While in his possession, the house served as a local tavern and store and as rooms provided to British officers.

When Spain regained control of the city in 1783, Joseph Peavett and his wife, Mary, elected to stay in St. Augustine and continued to be successful in their business ventures. After Peavett's death, his widow married an Irish Catholic man, John Hudson. Unfortunately, her new husband lacked Peavett's business skills. Although she had her own income as a midwife, by 1790, she was forced to put the house up for auction.

A Spanish colonial uniform in one of the downstairs rooms of the González-Alvarez House. *Author's original image.*

The house was purchased for the price of 942 pesos by a twenty-five-year-old immigrant from northwest Spain, Gerónimo Alvarez. He worked as a baker for the hospital when he first arrived in St. Augustine but had opened a store and earned enough money to take a wife two years prior to purchasing the house. At the time of purchase, the property also contained dove cotes, a chicken coop, two wells and an outbuilding kitchen. Alvarez made major alterations to the house, including the addition of several rooms and a framed porch.

Gerónimo Alvarez volunteered and served as a lieutenant during the Patriot Rebellion, although he was already fifty-three years old. Alvarez would also become the first mayor of St. Augustine in 1812 and once held a city council meeting in the house when the regular meeting room in the governor's house was locked due to the governor's absence.

After Gerónimo's death in 1846, the house was occupied by his son Antonio, who would himself serve two terms as mayor of St. Augustine. He and his descendants occupied the house until 1877.

The González-Alvarez House as it appeared under the ownership of Dr. Carver in 1895. Photo by Jack Boucher. *Courtesy of the Library of Congress Prints and Photographs Division, Washington, D.C.*

The second non-Spanish owner of the house was William B. Duke of New York, who purchased the house in 1880 for $2,000 and only kept the house for four years. In 1884, he sold it to Mrs. Mary Carver, a local dentist's wife, for $3,000. Dr. Carver installed paneling he purchased from a dismantled Presbyterian church and erected a round masonry tower on the northeast corner of the building.

Because so many of the city's visitors wanted to see his home, Dr. Carver began charging admission fees, marking the beginning of its history as a museum. The house made its first appearance as the "Oldest House" on a city directory map in 1885. By 1892, the first advertisement appeared, listing the house as open for visitors during the months of January, February and March.

The house was next purchased by James Henderson in early 1898 for the price of $10,000. It was operated by his wife as a showplace filled with antiques and curios, and she falsely identified the house to visitors as having once been the chapel of the monks who came to St. Augustine with Menéndez.

After his wife's death, Mr. Henderson sold the house to George Reddington, cofounder of the South Beach Alligator Farm and Museum of Marine Curios, which was the forerunner of today's St. Augustine Alligator Farm.

The St. Augustine Historical Society purchased the González-Alvarez House from Mr. Reddington in 1918 and now operates it as the centerpiece of their Oldest House Museum Complex. The interior of the house is furnished with period antiques. It is listed in the National Register of Historic Places and designated as a National Historic Landmark. The complex is open daily from 9:00 a.m. until 5:00 p.m., and guided tours of the González-Alvarez House are available every half hour.

THE FATHER O'REILLY HOUSE

B uilt during the First Spanish Period and believed to have been originally owned by Joachim de Florencia, this house located at 32 Aviles Street was purchased by Father O'Reilly in 1785 to serve as a rectory.

Born in Ireland while it was under British control and during the suppression of the Catholic faith, Michael O'Reilly received his religious education in Spain and took the name Miguel during his time there. After ordination, he came to Florida as the chaplain assigned to the Hibernia Regiment, which was comprised of Irish soldiers serving in the Spanish army. The regiment was unable to enter St. Augustine until the end of the Revolution due to a blockade of the British-held area.

Father O'Reilly's initial assignment in St. Augustine was as the chaplain to the Spanish troops serving there during the Second Spanish Period. One of the many sacraments he performed was the secret marriage of the governor's daughter, Dominga de Zespedes, to one of the Hibernia Regiment officers, Lieutenant Juan O'Donovan. O'Donovan was arrested for marrying without the permission of his commanding officer and sent to Havana for two years. Although the marriage was contested by Zespedes's family, it was eventually deemed legal and the couple was reunited.

Father O'Reilly was also the teacher of Cuban-born priest, writer and human rights activist Felix Varela, who is currently being considered for canonization as a Catholic saint. Father O'Reilly continued to serve as St. Augustine's parish priest until his death in 1812. In his will, he left instructions that the building was to serve as a home for nuns and be used as a school.

The Father O'Reilly House as it appeared in 1958. Photo by Jack Boucher. *Courtesy of the Library of Congress Prints and Photographs Division, Washington, D.C.*

In 1876, the house became the first convent of the Sisters of St. Joseph and the home of St. Joseph's Academy (1876–1920). At the request of Bishop Verot, who was the first bishop of the Diocese of St. Augustine, Mother Leocadie Broc selected eight sisters from the motherhouse in Le Puy, France, to be sent to Florida. Those selected for the mission were Sister Marie Sidonie Rascle, Superior and Sisters Marie Julie Roussel, Marie Josephine Deleage, Marie Clemence Freycenon, Saint Pierre Borie, Marie Joseph Cortial, Julie Clotilde Arsac and Marie Celenie Joubert.

The Sisters arrived in St. Augustine in early September 1866 with the assigned mission to educate the children of freed slaves, the only Europeans known to have come to this country for that purpose. Their long journey was not an easy one. After sailing across the Atlantic, they boarded a steamship that delivered them to the nearby town of Picolata. There, they found themselves unexpectedly divided for a night, as the mail wagon that was assigned to take them to St. Augustine could only provide seating for four passengers. The remaining four Sisters spent a second night aboard the steamship and were transported to their new home the following day.

Although they were provided with a building in which to live and teach, the Sisters arrived with no funding to begin their work. To support their mission, the Sisters made and sold French lace and also offered instruction in music, French language and lace making to the wives of wealthy visitors to the St. Augustine area. The mothers of their young African American students provided them with a steady supply of fresh fruits and vegetables from their own gardens and often helped the Sisters with chores. Their work was praised in the August 17, 1867 edition of the *St. Augustine Examiner*, which stated, "What they have done hitherto is a sure pledge of greater success in the future."

This prediction proved true as the Sisters opened seven schools within ten years and, by 1898, opened the two-story St. Cecilia's School in the African American community of Lincolnville. The Sisters of St. Joseph would continue to serve the community from the St. Cecilia's building until its closure in 1964. Today, it is the oldest surviving brick schoolhouse in the city. The St. Joseph Academy, which was founded by the Sisters in 1866, is the oldest continuously operating Catholic high school in the state of Florida.

The simple six-room, two-story Father O'Reilly House contains both original and reconstructed elements and has been continually used for religious purposes while under the ownership of the Sisters of St. Joseph. It has served as a school, a convent and a home for retired people.

The Sisters oversaw the restoration of the building in 2001. The downstairs area contains some of the equipment they used for lace making as well as samples of the lace they made. The upstairs rooms contain items that would have been used in the instruction of their students.

Among the items on display are two Madonna figures, which were gifts to the Sisters of St. Joseph. The Hurricane Lady, a four-foot-tall figure with a bisque head and hand attached to a redwood body, is dressed in a white gown and a golden lace Spanish mantilla. Legend has it that she was brought to this area aboard a Spanish cargo ship that encountered a hurricane while crossing the Atlantic in the late 1700s and that the ship's sailors prayed to her daily for safe passage. The second figure is known as the Pregnant Madonna. She is just over three and a half feet tall, carved from a single piece of wood and is believed to have been created in Belgium during the sixteenth century. She is simple in design, lacking any coloration or adornment, and stands with her hands clasped over her belly, as if she is instinctively protecting her unborn child.

"The Sewing Circle," from the First Coast Reflections project, Father O'Reilly House. *Author's original image.*

The Sisters of St. Joseph have operated the Father O'Reilly House, which is listed in the National Register of Historic Places, as a museum since the summer of 2003. It is open for tours Wednesdays through Saturdays. There is no admission fee, but donations to the Sisters are always welcome.

THE TOVAR HOUSE

The Tovar House, located at 22 St. Francis Street, is probably best known for the cannonball embedded in the exterior surface of one of its plaster-covered coquina walls. The cannonball is believed to have come from the 1740 British attack led by General James Oglethorpe.

Although Spanish infantryman Jose Tovar and his wife, Barbara Medina, were the first known owners of this house, very little is known about them. Other occupants prior to 1791 included a Scottish merchant named John Johnson during the British Period, followed by Jose Coruna, a Canary Islander, and an assistant surgeon named Tomas Caraballo after the Spanish regained control in 1784.

Gerónimo Alvarez purchased the house at public auction in the spring of 1791, and his heirs maintained control of the property until 1871. In a sketch of the Gonzáles-Alvarez House by artist Henry J. Morton, an Episcopal priest who visited the city of St. Augustine in March 1867, the Tovar House appears as a one-story structure with a hipped roof.

The next owner of the house was Frances M. von Balsom, who bought the property at a public auction in April 1871. She leased it to a Union brigadier general by the name of Martin D. Hardin, who resided in the Tovar House after the end of the Civil War. Hardin was originally from Illinois, the grandson of a United States senator and a family friend and protégé of Abraham Lincoln.

In March 1892, General Hardin hosted a ball in the house, and the following description appeared in a local newspaper:

Right: A 1700s cannonball embedded in an original coquina exterior wall at the Tovar House. *Author's original image.*

Below: The Tovar House as it appeared in 1961. *Courtesy of the Library of Congress Prints and Photographs Division, Washington, D.C.*

General Martin D. Hardin was a Tovar House resident after the end of the Civil War.
Courtesy of the Library of Congress Prints and Photographs Division, Washington, D.C.

The quaint old house of the General's one of the oldest if not the very oldest, has been repaired and made thoroughly comfortable without changing any of its distinguishing features, consequently the long room used for dancing had bare time-stained rafters, plain white walls, and the bare floor was dark with age. The other rooms and quaint old staircase are just as built three hundred years ago. At 11 the guests were ushered into the quaint old dining hall with stone floor, rafters black with age, old time mantel, where rows of candles were placed, improvised shelves around the room holding other candles that gave the prettiest light.[41]

General Hardin spent his last years living in St. Augustine. He died in December 1923 and was buried in the National Cemetery there.

The house was deeded to the South Beach Alligator Farm and Museum of Marine Curiosities in 1912 by Louis R. Hite, the only heir of Francis van Balsom. Just as was the case with the González-Alvarez House, the Tovar House was acquired by the St. Augustine Historical Society in 1918.

The house underwent extensive restoration and preservation work during 2012, including a fresh coat of lime-based whitewash made from oyster shells, just as would have been done when the house was first built. Temperature- and

"Morning Shadows," from the First Coast Reflections project, Tovar House. *Author's original image.*

humidity-control equipment was also installed to help protect the structure, but the components were carefully placed to help maintain the original character of the structure.

The Tovar House is part of the Oldest House Museum complex owned and operated by the St. Augustine Historical Society. It is open to visitors daily.

The historic gardens at the Cummer Museum of Art and Gardens, located on Riverside Avenue in Jacksonville. *Author's original image.*

The Kingsley Plantation House is the oldest plantation home in the state of Florida. *Author's original image.*

Above: The Major Webb House was built in the 1870s. The house is operated as a museum by the Mandarin Historical Society. *Author's original image.*

Left: The china cabinet inside the Major Webb House. *Author's original image.*

The Delius House, which was rediscovered more than fifty years after Delius moved away, is now located on the campus of Jacksonville University. *Author's original image.*

The Merrill House, which was built in 1886, is owned and operated by the Jacksonville Historical Society. *Author's original image.*

Above: The Foreman's House,
located in the Pablo Historical
Park at Jacksonville Beach,
was built by the FEC Railway
Company in 1900. *Author's
original image.*

Left: The wood-burning stove
in the kitchen of the Foreman's
House in Jacksonville Beach.
Author's original image.

Right: A rake used for harvesting oysters hangs by the back door in the kitchen of the Foreman's House. *Author's original image.*

Below: Courtyard view of the González-Alvarez House, which is the oldest house in the city of St. Augustine and the state of Florida. *Author's original image.*

Original family china in the upstairs dining room of the González-Alvarez House. *Author's original image.*

The Father O'Reilly House, located on Aviles Street in St. Augustine, was the original home of the Sisters of St. Joseph. *Author's original image.*

The Tovar House, also known as the cannonball house, is located on St. Francis Street in St. Augustine. *Author's original image.*

A courtyard view of the Peña-Peck House, which is owned by the city of St. Augustine and maintained by the Woman's Exchange. *Author's original image.*

An upstairs bedroom, with Peck family furnishings, in the Peña-Peck House. *Author's original image.*

The Peña-Peck House dining room with original Peck family furniture and china. *Author's original image.*

The Fernandez-Llambias House, located on St. Francis Street in St. Augustine, is owned by the St. Augustine Historical Society. *Author's original image.*

A courtyard view of the Ximenez-Fatio House, which is owned by the National Society of the Colonial Dames of America in the State of Florida. *Author's original image.*

"The Captain's Desk," from the First Coast Reflections project, Ximenez-Fatio House. *Author's original image.*

The Prince Murat House, located within the Dow Museum complex, was once home to the crown prince of Naples and nephew of Napoleon. *Author's original image.*

The Dow House is one of the oldest wooden structures in St. Augustine. *Author's original image.*

The Canova-de Medicis House, located within the Dow Museum property in St. Augustine. *Author's original image.*

The Howells House was once the winter home of writer William Dean Howells and his daughter, Mildred. *Author's original image.*

The Spear House was once a carriage house associated with the Spear Mansion hotel. *Author's original image.*

The Rose House was the home of rose expert Jean Gordon and housed the Rose Museum from 1956 until 1966. *Author's original image.*

The Worcester House, located within the Dow Museum property in St. Augustine. *Author's original image.*

The Carpenter's House was damaged during the Cuba-Florida Hurricane of 1944. *Author's original image.*

"The Kitchen Table," from the First Coast Reflections project, Carpenter's House. *Author's original image.*

The Clarke House, located in Orange Park, was built in 1912 and is the centerpiece of a beautiful community park. *Author's original image.*

The Dudley Farm House is one of eighteen historic buildings open to visitors in the Dudley Farm Historic State Park. *Author's original image.*

Above: The Marjorie Kinnan Rawlings House, which draws thousands of visitors to the rural area of Cross Creek each year. *Author's original image.*

Left: An architectural detail of a kitchen window in the Marjorie Kinnan Rawlings House. *Author's original image.*

THE PEÑA-PECK HOUSE

Juan Esteban de Peña arrived in the city of St. Augustine in 1742 to serve as the new royal treasurer, only to find that suitable housing was difficult to come by. The town had been raided and burned several times prior to his arrival. After four years of living in less than satisfactory conditions, he sought the assistance of Florida governor Manuel de Montiano, who petitioned King Philip V on his behalf. In 1750, the king of Spain ordered the construction of the structure now known as the Peña-Peck House, which stands today as one of the finest examples of First Spanish Period structures. The first floor and loggia are essentially the same today as they were when the house was originally constructed, with the exception of one dividing wall between the dining room and a space that now serves as the orientation center for visitors.

During the British Period, the house first served as the residence of Dr. John Moultrie, who would become governor of British East Florida in 1771. It was during his ownership of the house that four fireplaces and an east wing were added. His occupancy was followed by that of Governor Patrick Tonyn, who also used the house as the final seat of British government of the area until it was transferred back to the Spanish in 1784.

A 1790 survey of properties ordered by incoming Spanish governor Juan Nepomuceno de Quesada listed the house as being occupied by Joaquin Sanchez. It was put up for auction in 1791, and changed hands several times before being purchased by Francisco Xavier Sanchez. Sanchez was one of only two "Floridanos" who chose to stay in St. Augustine under British rule and had lived near the house all of his life. He never occupied the house. It served as rental property until his oldest daughter, Beatriz, married and moved into the house with her new husband, Francisco Perez.

In 1820, as Spanish rule of St. Augustine came to a close for the final time, the house was sold by the Sanchez heirs to José Mariano Hernández, who owned three local plantations and would later become the first delegate from the Florida Territory and the first Hispanic American to serve in the United States Congress. Although it is not known exactly how, Hernández lost control of the house in the late 1820s, and it again was sold several times before finally being purchased in 1837 by a Dr. Seth S. Peck of Whitesboro, New York.

Dr. Peck first visited St. Augustine in 1833 after reading a circular describing the health benefits of the area's climate in the treatment of those suffering from "consumption" and other pulmonary illnesses. Within a month of his arrival, two notices appeared in the *Florida Herald*—that Dr. Peck had "concluded to make this city his future residence" and that Dr. Andrew Anderson would be turning over his practice to Dr. Peck. He opened an office in the City Hotel several weeks later and moved his family

The Peña-Peck House as it appeared in 1936. Photo by Francis Benjamin Johnston. *Courtesy of the Library of Congress Prints and Photographs Division, Washington, D.C.*

to St. Augustine the following year. Sarah Peck and the couple's five children arrived aboard the schooner *Tropic* after a ten-day journey from New York in October 1834.

The Peck family took up residence at the Ximenez-Fatio Boarding House (which was then known as Mrs. Whitehurst's) after their arrival in St. Augustine. Following the death of their youngest daughter in June 1837, the family selected the "old Spanish treasury" building to serve as their new home and the location of Dr. Peck's medical practice because they liked the location, the old coquina walls and the large grounds.

The house had deteriorated badly over the years, so major repairs and alterations were needed before the family could move in and Dr. Peck could open his medical office on the ground floor. Much of the work was provided as "in kind" payment for medical services provided by Dr. Peck, though records indicate that he purchased doors, window glass, zinc and copper, flooring and a new front door with hardware. A second story was added to the structure and the remains of the east wing were demolished, returning the footprint of the house to its original L shape.

During the yellow fever epidemic of 1841 and just eight years after his arrival in St. Augustine, Dr. Seth Peck died. His family continued to live in the house, and his only son, John, began to practice medicine there in 1844. His youngest surviving daughter, Lucy, married a merchant from Vermont named George Burt. Their wedding took place in the house, on the evening of Tuesday, July 31, 1849. Although they chose to live in rented quarters elsewhere in the city, Lucy came "home" for the birth of her daughter, Anna Gardner Burt, in May 1850. It is believed that Anna was the only child ever to be born in the house, and she would also die in the house eighty-one years later.

Anna Gardner Burt, who never married, inherited the house upon the death of her aunt Mary in 1912. Ms. Burt was well known and dearly loved in the city and devoted much of her time to helping others. When Native Americans were imprisoned in the Castillo de San Marcos during the 1870s, she taught them English. Prior to her own death in 1931, Anna Burt made provisions in her will to provide care for indigent patients at Flagler Hospital and establish a scholarship fund at Rollins College in Winter Park. She also specified that the house should be given to the City of St. Augustine "to be maintained as an example of the old ante-bellum homes of the South."[12]

With its finances strained by the Depression, the city commission rejected the bequest in January of the following year. It was less than a week later that the Woman's Exchange of St. Augustine, of which Anna Burt had been a charter member, offered a proposal to assume responsibility for the structure. Public tours of the house began in May 1932 with an admission fee of twenty-five cents.

The house today is filled with Peck family furnishings, many of which are priceless antiques from the eighteenth century. The artwork on display includes pieces by nineteenth-century Florida artists Martin Johnson Heade, W. Staples Drown and Felix De Crano as well as two original Audubon colored engravings. During recent restoration work in the old kitchen, a fireplace that had been bricked over was opened up, revealing antique cast-iron cookware.

The Peña-Peck House, which has also been designated as a Florida Heritage Landmark, is located at 143 St. George Street, at the corner of Treasury Street. It is owned by the City of St. Augustine, and is operated as a museum by the Woman's Exchange of St. Augustine, which was founded in 1892 as a nonprofit organization. The Exchange of St. Augustine is one of only twenty remaining exchanges of the National Federation of Woman's Exchanges.

Guided tours of the house are available Sunday through Friday, between the hours of 12:30 p.m. and 4:00 p.m., and from 10:30 a.m. until 4:00 p.m. on Saturdays. The tours are free, although donations are always welcome.

THE FERNANDEZ-LLAMBIAS HOUSE

Dating from sometime during the First Spanish Period, the Fernandez-Llambias House is located at 31 St. Francis Street and serves as a fine example of the St. Augustine Plan architectural style. First constructed by Spanish craftsmen and later altered by British inhabitants, it exhibits the influence of both cultures in its architectural details.

When Florida was ceded by Spain to Great Britain in 1763, the house was a single-story coquina structure with only one room and a tabby floor and was owned by Pedro Fernandez. He was a native of Spain who married Josepha Baessa, whose family had lived in St. Augustine for several generations. As was the case with most residents of the area in 1763, they and their two children had to leave St. Augustine during the Spanish evacuation to Havana.

When the British took control of the city, the house had been sold to Jesse Fish, but the new officials refused to recognize the sale as legitimate. They chose to grant the house to Richard Henderson, who sold it to a Boston merchant named Thomas Adams. At some point during the British occupation, a second story and balcony were added to the structure and the downstairs was divided into two rooms. After the death of Thomas Adams, the house was sold to Nicholas Turnbull, the son of Dr. Andrew Turnbull, who was the founder of the New Smyrna colony located about seventy miles south of St. Augustine.

It is unknown if Nicholas Turnbull ever occupied the house because the sale took place just as the Spanish regained control of Florida, and Turnbull

The Fernandez-Llambias House as it appeared in 1936. Photo by Francis Benjamin Johnston. *Courtesy of the Library of Congress Prints and Photographs Division, Washington, D.C.*

elected to move to Georgia rather than become a subject of the Spanish Crown. Ownership of the property then reverted back to Jesse Fish, though it was left unattended until it was sold at public auction in 1790. A series of owners followed.

In spite of the improvements, the house once again went up for public auction in 1827 and was purchased by Benjamin Kendrick Pierce for just over $500. Benjamin was the brother of Franklin Pierce, who later became the fourteenth president of the United States. Benjamin Pierce enlisted as a lieutenant of artillery in the United States Army and, between the years of 1821 and 1842, was assigned to the areas of Pensacola and Micanopy as well as the area that would become known as Fort Pierce. Troops under his command erected a blockhouse constructed of palmetto logs near a freshwater spring along the banks of the Indian River in early January 1837. They named the blockhouse "Fort Pierce, after our worthy commander, Lt. Col. Benjamin Kendrick Pierce, commander of the First Regiment of Artillery."[43]

It wasn't until June 1854 that the house was purchased by Catalina Llambias, whose family would hold the property for the next sixty-five years. During the Civil War, Joseph Llambias was imprisoned for refusing to swear allegiance to the occupying Federal government. He was eventually released because of his advanced age. He and his wife were allowed to leave but required to abandon all of their possessions. When their son Joseph Francis Llambias returned to the home at the end of the war, he found it had been vandalized; the first floor had been used as a stable for the horses of Union soldiers.

The house remained in the Llambias family until it was sold to Harry Campbell in 1919. Mr. Campbell was an unmarried artist who was also the director of the Cape Cod School of Art and a summer resident of St. Augustine. While under his ownership, the house was rented out as a tearoom, gift shop and living quarters.

In 1932, Mr. Campbell sold the house to the three Newbill sisters— Annabel, Georgianna and Josephine. Josephine had been a Red Cross public health nurse and a member of the State Nurses Association Board of Directors in Galveston, Texas. Her sister Georgianna had been a public health nurse in Gainesville, Florida. Annabel was a social worker from the Nashville, Tennessee area. The three sisters kept the house as a private residence.

The Carnegie Institution of Washington purchased the house from the Newbill sisters in 1938 and gave it to the City of St. Augustine. Custodianship of the house was passed to the St. Augustine Historical Society in 1945.

The most recent restoration work at the Fernandez-Llambias House was overseen by the St. Augustine Restoration and Preservation Association during the 1950s. The extensive work

An architectural detail of wood pegs in the ceiling structure of the Fernandez-Llambias House. *Author's original image.*

was based on the findings of a study by a Cornell University architect, Stuart Moffett Barnette. He worked on the project for three years and later referred to the restoration of the Llambias House as "a pioneering venture in three ways" by citing the professional approach, the first-time attempt at the restoration of a Spanish house in the Southeast and the first major effort to organize historic documentation of Spanish colonial architecture. He further asserted that "as in all pioneering ventures many new and unexpected obstacles were met...There is no doubt that the solutions which were devised to overcome them can and will be improved upon in future undertakings of this nature."[44]

The Fernandez-Llambias House was named a National Historic Landmark in 1970, and has also been designated as a Florida Heritage Landmark. Although the house itself is not currently open to the public, use of the garden is available for private function rental through the St. Augustine Historical Society and is often used for weddings.

THE XIMENEZ-FATIO HOUSE

Archeological excavations indicate that the Aviles Street property on which the Ximenez-Fatio House now stands has been the site of European settlers' dwellings since as early as 1572. Previous homes were most likely constructed of a variety of materials including wattle and daub, post and thatch and tabby. No records exist to tell us who occupied these previous homes, though the artifacts recovered do lead historians to believe that these previous occupants were among the more affluent of early settlers.

One of the artifacts recovered on the Ximenez-Fatio House property is an extremely rare white-bronze Caravaca Cross, which was unearthed by archeologists in 2002. The cross was discovered along with ceramic artifacts that have been dated to the year 1650. This style of cross was named for a small town now known as Caravaca de la Cruz. The town, located near the River Argos in southeastern Spain, was given the title of "holy city" by the Vatican. This title has only been given to four other cities in the world. A Caravaca cross is identified by its double-armed design and is believed to attract good fortune while providing its wearer with protection from evil. Franciscan missionaries brought Caravaca crosses to the New World.

Unlike most of the surviving structures from the late colonial period, the Ximenez-Fatio House has seen very few structural alterations since its construction. It remains true to the intentions of its original builder and offers visitors an honest representation of its unique architectural legacy.

The Ximenez-Fatio House was built in 1798 by Andres Ximenez, a native of Ronda, Spain, who was married to Juana Pellicer, the daughter of Francisco and Margarita Femanias. Francisco Femanias was a master carpenter and was one of the New Smyrna colony refugees who relocated to St. Augustine.

The two-story house was constructed of coquina walls with a tabby floor, a wood roof and four dormer windows. The upper floor of the building served as the residence for the Ximenez family, while the lower section contained warehouse space and a general store. It is also believed that both a billiards room and tavern existed on the main floor. Sadly, Andres's wife, Juana, died in 1802, and he died just four years later.

The Ximenez heirs sold the house in 1830 to the recently widowed Margaret Cook of Charleston, South Carolina. She, with the assistance of Eliza Whitehurst, was the first person to operate the property as a boardinghouse. Up to twenty-four guests could be accommodated in the house, with rooms for single men located on the ground floor, while rooms for women and families were located upstairs.

In 1838, the property was sold to Sarah Petty Anderson, who hired Louisa Fatio to manage the business. Miss Fatio was a well-educated woman whose family plantation, New Switzerland, had recently been destroyed for a second time during an 1836 conflict with the Seminoles. William Bartram had visited the Fatio family's New Castle indigo plantation where her grandfather, Francis Philip Fatio, was the resident manager in 1774. He described the visit with these words:

> This very civil gentleman showed me his improvement. His garden is very neat and contains a greater variety than any other in the Colony. He has a variety of European Grapes imported from the Straight, Olives, Figs, Pomegranates, Filberts, Oranges, Lemons, and a variety of garden flowers from Europe &c.[45]

Francis Philip Fatio was one of the First Coast area's most successful and wealthy planters. His New Switzerland plantation encompassed ten thousand acres that produced indigo and rice and contained fruit tree orchards and citrus groves. The plantation home was a two-story structure with piazzas, balconies and rooms for entertaining guests. He was a scholarly man who spoke six languages. One wing of the house contained the family's library, which included works in English, French and Italian. Outbuildings included a kitchen with brick chimney and oven, a carriage house, a workshop for carpenters and blacksmiths and a small hospital to care for injured laborers.

The New Switzerland plantation was burned to the ground during the Patriot Rebellion, and the Fatio family moved to Fernandina in 1812. There, Louisa met and became engaged to a British naval officer, but he died before their wedding. She never married. The plantation was rebuilt, and the family returned to New Switzerland in 1824. Louisa had assumed management of the plantation by 1831, as both her father and stepmother had died. Not long after the 1836 attack by the Seminoles, she took the opportunity to move to St. Augustine.

Due in large part to her exceptional skills, which included the ability to speak four languages, Louisa Fatio earned enough money to purchase the house in 1855. Under her proprietorship, the boardinghouse became one of the city's most respected establishments, providing lodging for traveling tourists as well as invalids suffering from pulmonary diseases. Although her business suffered during the Civil War years, it recovered quickly, and she continued to operate the boardinghouse until her death in 1875. Her heirs sold the house to the National Society of the Colonial Dames of America in the State of Florida in 1939.

The house contains nine rooms on each floor and is furnished with items appropriate to the Territorial and Early Statehood Periods. The dining

A street-front view of the Ximenez-Fatio House as it appeared in the 1850s. *Courtesy of the National Society of the Colonial Dames of America in the State of Florida.*

"The Lady's Room," from the First Coast Reflections project, Ximenez-Fatio House. *Author's original image.*

room table is set for a three-course midday meal. Above the table is a *punkah*, which is a type of hand-operated fan designed to keep insects off of the food being served.

In the guest rooms, even the smallest of details has been carefully selected for historical accuracy. A foot warmer and bed warmer can be found by the fireplace in a room known as the Frail Lady Room, which was specifically set up for female visitors from the North who came to recuperate in St. Augustine's warm climate. An astral lamp, designed with a ring-shaped oil reservoir to prevent shadows being cast, sits on the center table in the upstairs Owner's Parlor. This room in the morning hours is dappled with light reflected by its prisms catching the sunlight from the nearby open balcony doors. The Sea Captain's Room contains nautical instruments beside the inkwell and quill on the desk.

The original wide fireplace and beehive oven have both been preserved in the detached kitchen building, which holds the distinction of being the only remaining eighteenth-century freestanding kitchen in St. Augustine.

Located at the corner of Aviles and Cadiz Streets, the Ximenez-Fatio House is listed in both the National Register of Historic Places and the Historic American Buildings Survey. It has also been designated as a Florida Heritage Landmark.

The Ximenez-Fatio House is owned and operated as a museum by the National Society of the Colonial Dames of America in the State of Florida. The mission of the Colonial Dames is to acquire, restore and interpret historic properties that offer opportunities to experience America's heritage. Guided tours of the home are available Tuesdays through Saturdays.

THE PRINCE MURAT HOUSE

Considered by many to be among the oldest surviving Colonial homes in St. Augustine, it is believed that the Prince Murat House located at 250 St. George Street was built in 1815 by Antonio Huertas on a lot he purchased from Antonio Canova. Canova purchased the house from Huertas in 1821. The one-and-a-half story coquina house, with its distinctive pink plaster exterior and side-gable balcony, was owned by various members of the Canova family until 1877.

The Prince Murat House is named after its most famous occupant, Prince Achille Murat, who was crown prince of Naples and a nephew of Napoleon Bonaparte. After Napoleon was exiled a second time and Murat's father was dethroned and executed by his own subjects in 1815, the young prince was exiled to Austria with his mother and siblings. Achille was granted permission to immigrate to the United States when he turned twenty-one years of age in 1822. He befriended Richard Call, Florida's territorial delegate to Congress, while visiting Washington, D.C. It was Call who convinced Murat that there were ample opportunities available in the territory of Florida.

It is not known exactly when Prince Murat occupied the house, but historians date his arrival in St. Augustine to the spring of 1824. During his time there, which lasted through the 1830s, he served as a bondsman for the city treasurer. He also joined the militia and the Masonic society. He was active in local politics until he was accused of fraudulent voting in an election. He also is known to have purchased almost three thousand acres of land about ten miles south of St. Augustine, where he started a plantation.

The Prince Murat Coffee House, as it appeared in 1937. *Courtesy of the Library of Congress Prints and Photographs Division, Washington, D.C.*

Murat was also known for his somewhat odd behavior, such as his willingness to eat baked turkey buzzard, boiled owl, roasted crow, stewed alligator, lizards and rattlesnakes. Murat had a curious aversion to water, taken either internally or externally. He said that water was intended only for the beasts of the field, and he never drank it without adding whisky to it. It was also noted that although he had an aversion to bathwater, he would occasionally cover his head with mosquito netting and then lower himself into the Matanzas River.

Murat bought land for a second plantation approximately fifteen miles east of Tallahassee in 1825 and became the mayor of Tallahassee that same year. There, he met and married a sixteen-year-old widow named Catherine Daingerfield Willis Gray. Catherine was the daughter of Colonel Byrd Willis and, on her mother's side, a grandniece of George Washington.

Prince Murat and his new wife made their home in Tallahassee, but he continued to make periodic visits to St. Augustine, and it was there in 1926 that he met and developed a close friendship with the writer Ralph Waldo Emerson. Emerson, who at the age of twenty-three was two years younger than Murat, came to St. Augustine aboard a sloop out of Charleston, South

Carolina, seeking a warmer climate for treatment of his tuberculosis. The two men shared their thoughts on a number of topics, and Emerson referred to Murat as "a philosopher, a scholar, a man of the world, very skeptical but very candid, and an ardent lover of truth."[46]

During his time in St. Augustine, Murat began to write essays on the topics of American politics and daily life in Florida. The former prince was fascinated by American democracy and liberty, writing in his collection of essays entitled "Letters from the United States," "It is the American Union which gives us the best model of government."

Murat also served as a translator and included this "Note of Translator" at the end of a Spanish "Royal Order" document that was originally written in 1815:

> *N.B. These Spanish documents are most wretchedly copied: so much so, as many times to render them perfectly unintelligible, and many other times, which is still worse, to make the sense entirely different from the one intended. This, of course, I could not correct, without departing from the fidelity of a translator; but I wish to have it clearly understood that I am not accountable for the nonsense and contradictions contained in the foregoing pages.*[47]

"Letters Home," from the First Coast Reflections project, Prince Murat House. *Author's original image.*

After the 1830 revolution in France, Murat returned to Europe in hopes of regaining some of his family's lost fortune. He returned to Florida in 1834 after all his efforts proved unsuccessful. He and his wife moved from Tallahassee to a small plantation in Jefferson County, Florida, where he continued to live until his death in 1847.

The Prince Murat House passed through a series of owners between 1877 and the late 1930s, including John P. Howard and Amos C. Spear. The structure housed a small restaurant known as the Prince Murat Coffee House during the 1930s, and Greta Garbo is said to have dined on avocados there in 1939.

Kenneth Worcester Dow, a lumber and real estate businessman originally from Detroit, purchased the house in 1940, and it eventually became the cornerstone of the Dow Museum of Historic Houses. Mr. Dow, whose passions included art and antique collecting, traveled extensively and furnished the Murat House with French Napoleonic Era antiques.

The Prince Murat House is one of nine historic homes included in the Dow Museum complex, which is owned and operated by the Daytona Museum of Arts and Sciences. The Dow Museum entrance is located at 149 Cordova Street, and the complex is open to visitors until 5:00 p.m. seven days a week.

THE DOW HOUSE

The Dow House was built in 1839 by Antonio Canova for his son, Paul. It is one of the few wooden structures from that time period still standing in the city. Canova used the Murat House as a template for the layout of rooms in the Dow House.

This Florida Territorial Period house was originally located on St. George Street and was moved to its current location in 1909 at the request of Mary Hayden, an affluent widow who also ordered the construction of two winter cottages for visitors to St. Augustine. A separate kitchen building, which was originally attached to the rear of the house, was also moved and reattached to the west end of the building.

The house frame is built with the use of wooden pegs and is constructed of straight-sawn heart of pine lumber. There are Greek Revival corner blocks on the two dormers and ornamental brackets that support the door cap. The exterior siding is beaded weatherboard, most unusual for the St. Augustine area.

Kenneth Dow was the only son of a wealthy Michigan family who made their fortune in the lumber business. He was also a World War II army veteran, who spent most of his life traveling the world and collecting art, antiques and unusual objects. He moved to the St. Augustine area in the late 1940s. He and his wife, Mary Mohan Dow, were among the first citizens of St. Augustine to recognize the importance of preservation. In 1989, he donated the vast majority of his collection, including the houses that now comprise the Dow Museum of Historic Houses, to the Daytona

Kenneth Worcester Dow, standing by the Spanish gates at the Murat House. *Courtesy of the Dow Museum of Historic Houses and the Museum of Arts and Sciences, Daytona Beach.*

Beach Museum of Arts and Sciences. His impressive collection of American fine art and decorative arts, which spans a time period of more than three hundred years, is now housed in the four-thousand-square-foot Kenneth Worcester Dow and Mary Mohan Dow Gallery of American Art at the Museum of Art and Science in Daytona Beach.

Dow purchased the house from a widow named Sarah McKinnon in 1941. McKinnon was born in Dublin, Ireland, on May 16, 1843, though her family moved to the town of Trenton in the Ontario area of Canada when she was still an infant. She came to St. Augustine in 1884 when her husband, Killian McKinnon, landed a two-year contract to work on the construction of Henry Flagler's grand Ponce de Leon Hotel. The couple

The house in the foreground of this 1902 photograph is the Murat House. Next to it is the Dow House, in its original St. George Street location. *Courtesy of State Archives of Florida, Florida Memory, http://floridamemory.com/items/show/31736.*

had five children. At the time of the sale to Mr. Dow, she was St. Augustine's oldest surviving resident; a clause was included that allowed her to continue to live in the house. She took up painting when she was 100 years old and continued to reside in the house until her death at the age of 103.

The Dow House is one of nine historic homes included in the Dow Museum of Historic Houses complex, which is owned and operated by the Daytona Museum of Arts and Sciences. The Dow Museum entrance is located at 149 Cordova Street, and the complex is open to visitors until 5:00 p.m. seven days a week.

THE CANOVA-DE MEDICIS HOUSE

Antonio Canova, an emigrant from the island of Minorca, originally built this coquina house for his family on a lot located at 46 Bridge Street in 1840, during the Territorial Period and the time of the Seminole Wars. The house was deeded to his son Ramon in 1866 in a transaction that was recorded as stating the price as "$1.00 and love and affection" in the official deed book.[48] The house passed to his heirs until it was sold to Colonel Albert Tracy in 1878. Colonel Tracy gave a quitclaim deed to Amos C. Spear that same year, and it was almost immediately sold to Mollie H. Pease.

In 1899, the house became the home of Emanuel de Medicis, who was the grandson of Elias de Medicis of Corsica and Tecla Marin of Minorca, who arrived at New Smyrna in 1768. He was the owner of a dry goods, clothing and hat store on Charlotte Street. Emanuel converted the structure into a boardinghouse and also built the Star General Store building to house his business. By 1921, the building that once housed the store had been divided into apartments for the families of two of his seven daughters. The Canova-de Medicis House, to which a second story had been added, was deeded to de Medicis's nephew, John L. Henry.

The ground-floor walls of this six-room, two-story house were constructed of coquina blocks laid in horizontal courses and plastered on both the interior and exterior surfaces. One original nine-over-six-light, double-hung wooden sash is located on the east wall of the larger room downstairs, near the staircase. The wood-frame second floor is sided with wood weatherboard and novelty siding. The house also features angled flush boards in the

Above: The Canova-de Medicis House, as it appeared in 1961. Photo by Prime A. Beaudoin. *Courtesy of the Library of Congress Prints and Photographs Division, Washington, D.C.*

Right: An architectural detail of the exposed coquina blocks inside the Canova-de Medicis House. *Author's original image.*

dormer. The northern and western additions were constructed sometime between 1885 and 1894.

The Canova-de Medicis House is the third-oldest structure in the Dow Museum of Historic Houses complex, which is owned and operated by the Daytona Museum of Arts and Sciences. The Dow Museum entrance is located at 149 Cordova Street, and the complex is open to visitors until 5:00 p.m. seven days a week.

THE HOWELLS HOUSE

The Howells House was built in 1907 under the direction of Mary Hayden to serve as a winter rental cottage, although the term "cottage" seems inappropriate for the large Colonial Revival–style house.

The house is named after William Dean Howells. Howells, a close friend of Mark Twain, was a writer as well as the editor of *Atlantic Monthly* from 1871 to 1881. He and his daughter, Mildred, had visited St. Augustine several times between the years 1915 and 1918. They resided in the house at 246 St. George Street during the winter of 1916.

To his editor at *Harper's*, Howells referred to St. Augustine as a "dear old town" and seemed especially charmed by the peach blossoms and mockingbirds of the area. In a letter to a friend written during his 1916 stay, Howells wrote of the St. Augustine winter weather:

> We have been having a beautiful summer which the almanac would call winter, but with only five days of frostless cold…so far. Much of the time we have fervently desired the shadow, as we walked to our lunch at the Italian trattoria across the plaza up St. George Street.[49]

In his article titled "A Confession of St. Augustine," he wrote of his admiration for the town's warm winter weather:

> The Floridian winter, which is not a season but merely an incident of the year-long summer of the latitude, seldom arrives from New York or Boston, but arrives from Chicago by way of Chattanooga.[50]

In the same article, he wrote of the small-town charm of the city:

As for the allure of St. Augustine itself, it was largely that of all small cities not densely built over their area, and it kept the tradition of a country town in dooryards with flowers, and back yards with homely vegetables, and here and there a vacant lot where the sweet corn and pea vines flourished, not remote from the centers of commerce and fashion which, as I have said, do not intermit their business or pleasure on Sundays.[51]

After that visit to the city of St. Augustine, Howells published an article in *Harper's Magazine* that described the city at the peak of its filmmaking era:

St. Augustine is indeed the setting...[for] companies of movie players rehearsing their pantomimes everywhere....No week passes without encountering these genial fellow creatures dismounting from motors...or delaying in them to darken an eye or redden lip or cheek or pull a bodice

The author William Dean Howells in 1908. *Courtesy of the Library of Congress Prints and Photographs Division, Washington, D.C.*

into shape before alighting to take part in the drama. I talk as if there were no men in these affairs but there were plenty…villains like brigands or smugglers or savages, with consoling cowboys or American cavalrymen for the rescue of ladies in extremity. Seeing the films so much in formation we naturally went a great deal to see them ultimate in movie theaters, where we found them all nearly bad.[52]

Howells had begun to write a novel set in St. Augustine titled *The Home-Towners*, but it was not yet completed when he died in 1920. In it, when a main character named Rayburn arrives by train and is being driven to a hotel, Howells offered this description that still rings true today:

They drove up the street colonnaded with palmettos, past the summer cottages, and the dooryards with cedars and magnolias and the burning red of poinsettia flowers at the verandas, and then a center where suddenly the architectural presence ceased to be domestic and American, and became Andalusian and dramatic; with walls and roofs of warm color, and gateways of garden closes where fountains played.[53]

The Howells House serves as the administrative offices for the Dow Museum of Historic Houses museum staff and is not currently open to the public.

THE SPEAR HOUSE

The story of the Spear House is, in some respects, a story of loss. The Spear House was built as a single-story structure in 1899. It is believed to have been the carriage house for the Spear Mansion, a large and luxurious hotel that was once located on the adjacent property at 242 St. George Street. Given its elongated rectangular exterior shape and the unusual structure of its interior, one can easily imagine it housing turn-of-the-century carriages.

The Spear Mansion was built by a former Union army officer, Captain Thomas F. House, who also built the Lorrillard Villa and the Sunnyside Hotel. The mansion first served as a winter home for John P. Howard of Vermont, a man who made a substantial amount of money in the hotel business and who traveled extensively. Mr. Howard never married, so the mansion was eventually passed to his sister Catherine Maria, who had married Amos C. Spear. It is believed that her daughter, Julia Spear, was the first person to operate the mansion as a hotel.

The Spear Mansion property was purchased by the Sisters of St. Joseph in 1938, and the mansion was demolished. Since the carriage house had already been sold to the de Medicis family, it was not included in the sale. Today, the Spear House is all that remains of the Spear Mansion legacy.

The carriage house was purchased by John Henry, nephew of Emanuel de Medicis, who wanted to convert the structure into a home for his new wife, Marie Louise. Their time in the house would be limited, however, as she came from a prominent family, and they were not pleased with the idea of their daughter residing in a carriage house.

The Spear Mansion, which was demolished in 1938. From a photonegative of an Ed Mueller postcard. *Courtesy of State Archives of Florida, Florida Memory, http://floridamemory.com/ items/show/147919.*

A section of hand-painted wall mural uncovered during restoration of the Spear House. *Author's original image.*

A second story and porch were added in 1910, after the Henry family had moved into the Worcester House. The Spear House was divided into separate units during the 1920s and used as a boardinghouse. Additionally, it was further modified to serve as an apartment building until it was purchased by Kenneth Dow sometime between 1941 and 1950.

The Spear House is located within the Dow Museum of Historic Houses complex, which is owned and operated by the Daytona Museum of Arts and Sciences. The Dow Museum entrance is located at 149 Cordova Street, and the complex is open to visitors until 5:00 p.m. seven days a week.

THE ROSE HOUSE

The second of two winter rental cottages that Mary Hayden had built in 1907, this two-story home contains elements of both the Carpenter Gothic and Colonial Revival styles.

The Rose House is best known for housing a rose museum owned by Jean Wickham Reilly from 1956 until 1966. She was a member of the American Rose Society and organized national rose exhibitions in the United States. She also wrote articles and rose-themed books including *Pageant of the Rose*; *Rose Recipes: Customs, Facts, Fancies*; and *Immortal Roses: One Hundred Rose Stories* under the pen name of Jean Gordon. In an interesting excerpt from her 1953 book, *Pageant of the Rose*, she noted the unusual medicinal use of rose hips during the Second World War:

> *During World War II when the supply of citrus fruits had been cut off, some of this rose lore proved to be valuable to British chemists. After exhaustive tests they determined that rose hips have a vitamin C content 400 per cent greater than that of oranges. Following this discovery the British government instituted a campaign during the autumn of 1941 that led to one of the greatest medicinal uses of the rose in modern times. In Scotland alone, women and Boy Scouts collected approximately 200 tons of the bitter red fruit of the dog rose, the commonest hedge rose in the British Isles. It has been estimated that this harvest represented 134,000,000 individual hips, which were converted into syrup.*[54]

The front porch and entry of the Rose House, probably photographed during the late 1960s. *Courtesy of the Dow Museum of Historic Houses and the Museum of Arts and Sciences, Daytona Beach.*

Ms. Gordon selected the city for the location of her museum based on St. Augustine's status as the nation's oldest city and the widely held belief that roses are among the oldest of flowers. Her House of Roses museum, which opened in 1956, displayed items made from china, glass, wood, metal, fabric, crystal and stone that featured roses.

Her collection, which was exhibited at the Brooklyn Botanic Gardens and the Smithsonian Institute in Washington prior to the opening of her St. Augustine museum, included an ivory statue from the Orient, a jewel box from France, gold-brocade fabric with red silk roses, bronze roses created by German craftsmen and Tudor rose items from England. She also displayed more common items such as stamps from many countries featuring roses, rose-shaped items such as buttons and butter molds and rose-patterned dinnerware. Her collection was bequeathed to the New York Botanical Society in 1975.

The Rose House is part of the Dow Museum of Historic Houses. It now is home to a gallery displaying the work of local artists in the ground-floor rooms and several working artists' studio spaces in the upstairs rooms. The Dow Museum entrance is located at 149 Cordova Street, and the complex is open to visitors until 5:00 p.m. seven days a week.

THE WORCESTER HOUSE

This two-and-a-half-story Richardson Romanesque frame house was constructed in 1906 by John Henry for his wife, Marie Louise, to provide her with a more stylish home than the Spear House. This type of architecture is named after Henry Hobson Richardson and was most popular between the years of 1880 and 1900. Richardson Romanesque buildings typically feature substantial use of stonework, semicircular arched windows and hipped roof structures.

The home originally had a curved, single-story covered porch that wrapped around from the side to the front of the building. By the time Kenneth Dow purchased the house in 1949, the half of the porch's roof that faced Cordova Street had deteriorated so badly that it had to be removed. Mr. Dow also had the house divided, and his aunt, Susan Alice Worcester, occupied one of the two apartments. Dow, who was an only child, had a very close relationship with Ms. Worcester as his parents had both passed away when he was in his twenties. Today, the house still bears her name.

Although most of the original arched windows have been replaced, an effort to maintain the character was made by preserving the arch detail when the new windows were installed. An original stained-glass window in the stairwell has been preserved. The fireplace in the dining room is also original and especially lovely with its beautiful tiles, rich wood mantle and antique mirror. Additionally, the interior of the house is filled with Edwardian furnishings and period-appropriate touches such as gas lighting and a coal-burning stove.

Above: The Richardson Romanesque Worcester House, prior to renovations that did not permit preserving the original character of the house. *Courtesy of the Dow Museum of Historic Houses and the Museum of Arts and Sciences, Daytona Beach.*

Opposite: Entry door and window details of the Worcester House, which provide evidence of the former Richardson Romanesque elements. *Author's original image.*

The Worcester House is located within the Dow Museum of Historic Houses complex, which is owned and operated by the Daytona Museum of Arts and Sciences. The Dow Museum entrance is located at 149 Cordova Street, and the complex is open to visitors until 5:00 p.m. seven days a week.

THE CARPENTER'S HOUSE

John Henry built this house in 1909 using materials left over after the construction of the Spear and Worcester Houses. The Carpenter's House was intended to provide a home for his wife's widowed sister, Alberta Johnson, and her two daughters. Mrs. Johnson would later serve in a variety of positions with the Florida Historical Society, which was founded in St. Augustine in 1856.

The two-story house leans, but still stands, after taking heavy damage and becoming detached from its foundation during a late-season hurricane in October 1944.

The storm, which is known as the Cuba-Florida Hurricane, was a category-four hurricane with winds above 160 miles per hour when it struck the island of Cuba before accelerating and making landfall on the southwest coast of Florida near Sarasota and then crossing the state before making its way back out to sea by passing through St. Augustine.

When the storm arrived in St. Augustine on the afternoon of October 19, winds were still above ninety miles per hour, and heavy rains had been falling all day. Residents were warned by radio to evacuate low-lying areas, and between six and seven hundred took shelter in the Ponce de Leon Hotel. Another four to five hundred people found shelter at the City Building and the Civic Center. Residents of Vilano Beach were evacuated by trucks from Palm Valley. Local businesses offered use of ambulance, trucks, a bus and road equipment. Weather updates for the city were provided by a coast guardsman named Emery Stevens, who courageously stood watch in the

Flooding at the foot of the Bridge of Lions in St. Augustine during the 1944 Cuba-Florida Hurricane. *Courtesy of State Archives of Florida, Florida Memory, http://floridamemory.com/items/ show/141389.*

tower of the lighthouse throughout the storm. When it was over, the city's pier had been cut in half by the pounding waves, numerous trees were down, flood damage was widespread and, tragically, two people had lost their lives—a student at the Naval Academy had ventured into the water near the causeway, and a man who worked at the academy went in to rescue him. Both men drowned.

The Carpenter's House is part of the Dow Museum of Historic Houses. Due to the structural damage sustained during the hurricane, the Carpenter's House is not open for visitors, but the downstairs areas can be viewed through the open doors. The Dow Museum entrance is located at 149 Cordova Street, and the complex is open to visitors until 5:00 p.m. seven days a week.

ORANGE PARK

Orange Park is located on the western banks of the St. Johns River in Clay County, approximately fifteen miles south of Jacksonville. A British land grant, issued to James Crisp in 1769 by House of Lords member the Earl of Egmont, included plans for a sixteen-house village and the promise of the advance of a cow and a sow for each settler. The five-thousand-acre Upper Crisp grant encompassed the area that would eventually become Fleming Island and Orange Park. Records related to this enterprise have been lost, but it is believed that attacks on plantations in the area disrupted the plans.

The first known settlers in the area were William and Rebecca Pengree, who received a two-thousand-acre land grant from the governor in the year 1776. They left the plantation in 1783 when Florida returned to Spanish rule but returned in 1787 and stayed until 1794. After William's death in 1803, Rebecca sold the land to Zephaniah Kingsley, who established the Laurel Grove plantation there. Kingsley left the area and moved to Fort George Island at the end of the Patriot Rebellion, selling Laurel Grove to John Houston McIntosh in 1817. McIntosh further developed the plantation by adding a sawmill and a sugar mill. In 1867, the plantation was rented to Harriet Beecher Stowe, though she would soon choose to make her winter home across the St. Johns River in the community of Mandarin.

The town of Orange Park was founded in 1877 when Washington Gano Benedict purchased almost nine thousand acres of land, including the former Laurel Grove Plantation. He founded the Florida Winter Home

Improvement Company and launched an innovative advertising campaign that included a fifteen-by-two-hundred-foot billboard on the banks of the St. Johns River. He soon began selling lots of various sizes, each of which included its own orange tree. Benedict also laid out the streets—including Kingsley Avenue, River Road and Plainfield Avenue. In 1879, the town of Orange Park, with a total of twenty-six qualified voters, was incorporated. Large resort hotels such as the Marion, the Park View and the Sparhawk were constructed, and a twelve-hundred-foot dock was built to lure visiting Northern tourists traveling aboard the river's steamboats.

Orange Park maintained its small-town character for many years. When the Johnson family, founders of the Palmolive Soap Company, began construction of their Mira Rio estate on Astor Street in 1922, the town had no electrical service. The Johnsons had an artesian well dug and used it to operate a turbine and generate power to provide lighting for the large residence. By 1937, the Clay Electric Cooperative was formed, and electrical service became much more commonplace. The house is now the home of the Club Continental, which offers a private dining and tennis club as well as one of the area's most romantic hotels. It is also available for event rental.

The Winterbourne Inn, a historic plantation-style structure built in 1874, is located just around the corner from the Club Continental on Winterbourne West and today also serves as a special-events venue. Originally, it was the home the Johnson family rented and eventually purchased from Washington Benedict prior to the construction of the Mira Rio estate.

Other historic homes in the area include the William Helffrich House on Stiles Avenue, which was built in 1882 by a German minister from Philadelphia who was nearing retirement, and the 1,250-square-foot, two-story Joseph Green House on McIntosh Avenue. It was built in 1893 by an African American settler from Mississippi and is the oldest documented building associated with Orange Park's African American heritage. Both of these privately owned homes are listed in the National Register of Historic Places, but are not open for tours.

The River Road Historic District is located at the junction of River Road and Stiles Avenue, slightly less than a mile north of the Club Continental. The district contains ten historic buildings, which are currently private homes and not open to the public. Other historic districts located within what is now Clay County include the Memorial Home Community Historic District in Penney Farms, the Middleburg Historic District and the Green Cove Springs Historic District.

In spite of its small-town appearance, between the years 1930 and 1965, Orange Park became home to a center for biological and behavioral research when Yale University, the Rockefeller Foundation and the Carnegie Foundation funded the establishment of the Yale Laboratories for Primate Biology. Dr. Robert M. Yerkes, who received a doctorate in psychology in 1902 from Harvard University, was a distinguished professor of psychobiology at Yale University when he established the center. Dr. Yerkes based his research on the premise that primates, because of their evolutionary closeness to humans, could shed the most light on the roots of human behavior. The center was purchased by Emory University in 1956 and was relocated to their campus in Atlanta in 1965. The land once occupied by the research center is now a development known as Foxwood.

Much like the community of Mandarin, the opening of the three-mile-wide Buckman Bridge in 1970 brought an explosive growth to Orange Park. The once-rural community is now a city unto itself.

THE CLARKE HOUSE

Originally from Bury-St. Edmonds, England, William Clarke moved to Jacksonville, Florida, after his discharge from the Union army at the end of the Civil War and established the Old Reliable Plumbing Company. He married Fannie Dawkins and their son, William Francis, was born in 1884.

William Francis Clarke married Carrie S. Kellogg sometime between 1905 and 1907. In 1908, Carrie gave birth to their son, William Edward. Mr. Clarke purchased thirty acres of land near his wife's parents' home in Orange Park and built the two-story, tin-roofed house in 1912 to provide his only son with a place to hunt, fish, ride horses and engage in other "wholesome" activities.

William Francis Clarke commuted to Jacksonville each day and continued to run his father's plumbing business, though he was very active in the Orange Park community affairs. He served as a member of the town council and was elected mayor in the late 1920s.

Clarke's wife, Carrie, tended the kitchen garden and, with the help of hired hands, began the planting of pecan trees. Clarkes' Pecans proved to be a successful business venture, and their product was shipped by railroad and sold worldwide bearing the stamp of "Clarke Pecan Farm—Orange Park, Florida."

During the 1940s, an apartment located on the Clarke farm was the home of one of the Yerkes Laboratory researchers, Keith Hayes; his wife, Cathy; and a young chimpanzee named Viki. As she grew older, Viki discovered

Carrie & Billy Clarke
1621 Main St.   2/1/13 -

ways to escape from the confines of the apartment and would often visit the Clarke home, sometimes amusing herself by taking laundry from the clothesline and using it to decorate the nearby pecan trees.

Carrie Clarke was active in the Orange Park Garden Club and the Orange Park Woman's Club, a strong supporter of Baptist Children's Home and an American Red Cross volunteer, as well as a member of the Daughters of the American Revolution. As a devout Baptist, she would drive her car through the small town each Sunday morning to pick up children for the Sunday classes she held on her front porch. She also assisted in the purchase of the property at the corner of Kingsley Avenue and Astor Street for the construction of the First Baptist Church. It was well known that young women whose

Above: *Remembered Romance*, from the First Coast Reflections project, Clarke House. *Author's original image.*

Opposite: Mrs. Carrie Clarke and her son, William, in 1913. *Courtesy of the Historical Society of Orange Park.*

families needed assistance with wedding receptions could count on her to not only provide her home as a location but also to bake a wedding cake for the couple.

The Clarkes' only son, Bill, studied at Stetson University and obtained his chiropractor's license, but returned to the family's plumbing business, which he ran until shortly before his death in 1963. His widow, Georgia, continued to live in the home until it was purchased by the City of Orange Park in 1991.

The Clarke House is located on the grounds of the Clarke House Park at 1039 Kingsley Avenue in Orange Park. It has been listed in the National Register of Historic Places since 1998.

The Clarke House is open to the public for Carrie Clarke Day, held annually on the third Saturday in March, and on Veterans Day. There is also an open house during the Town of Orange Park's annual Holiday in the

"The Source of Light," from the First Coast Reflections project, Clarke House. *Author's original image.*

Park, usually held on the first Saturday in December. The Historical Society of Orange Park conducts its meetings in the Clarke House at 6:30 p.m. on the second Monday of each month, with the exception of July. All meetings are open to the public.

GAINESVILLE AREA

Hernando de Soto was the first European to visit the Alachua County area of Florida when his army passed through in August 1539, but it would be more than one hundred years before the Spanish colonists set up the first cattle ranches in the Paynes Prairie area. They used Timucuan laborers to help them manage the herds. The largest ranch came to be known as Hacienda de la Chua, a name derived from the Timucuan word "Chua" (which translated to "sinkhole") preceded by the Spanish article "la." This is believed to be the source of the name for the Alachua band of the Seminole tribe that settled in the region in the eighteenth century and for whom the county was named. The Hacienda de la Chua was owned by a Spaniard, Don Tomas Mendez Marquez, and operated from 1646 until it was destroyed by raiders from the Carolinas in 1706.

The first Spanish land grant in the area was given to Don Fernando de la Maza Arredondo, a merchant and resident of St. Augustine, by King Ferdinand VII of Spain in December 1817. Arredondo's grant was one of the largest in Florida history, totaling over 280,000 acres, and was given as a reward for Arredondo's assistance in raising troops to defend St. Augustine during the Patriot Rebellion.

After Florida was annexed to the United States in 1824, the small town of Newnansville became the seat of the newly founded Alachua County. The conversion of Florida from territory to statehood saw the arrival of new settlers and an expansion of agricultural activities in the Alachua County area. When plans were revealed that the new Florida

Railroad, which would provide service between the cities of Fernandina and Cedar Key, would bypass Newnansville, the county's residents voted to create a new town on the railroad line. This new town would also become the new county seat.

The colorful story of the founding of Gainesville actually begins at Boulware Springs, where in the summer of 1853, a group of settlers from various areas of the county held a meeting that is recorded as having been so contentious that fist fights nearly erupted. But tempers were calmed by some political vote swapping, and the name of Gainesville, in honor of Seminole Indian war general Edmund P. Gaines, was selected by the majority of those in attendance.

A site for the town, on Black Oak Ridge, was selected the following year, and sixty acres of land were purchased from Major James B. Bailey, a cotton plantation owner and former county treasurer. When the new railroad line was completed in 1859, it passed six blocks south of the new county courthouse. Surrounding the town square was the new city of Gainesville, neatly laid out in an eight-block gridiron and including the first school, which was built in 1856. By 1860, the town had its own general store, three hotels and slightly more than 250 residents.

In February 1864, a small Union raiding party occupied Gainesville. Five days later, the raiding party joined other Union troops in the Battle of Olustee, where they were defeated. A second Union attempt to take the city of Gainesville took place in August of that same year, and although the Union troops did manage to loot the city, they were driven from the area by Confederate troops after a battle that lasted less than two hours.

After the end of the Civil War, Union colonel Henry F. Dutton transformed Gainesville into one of the largest cotton shipping stations in the state. Colonel Dutton was the head of H.F. Dutton and Company, which he established in 1869, and of the second H.F. Dutton and Company, which was established in 1878. The development of agriculture in the area continued in the 1880s with the expansion of citrus and vegetable farming in Alachua County. By the 1890s, phosphate mining and lumbering had also become part of the local economic development. But the city of Gainesville was on the verge of taking on an entirely new role that would make it the center of higher education for the state.

In 1898, the city of Gainesville purchased Boulware Springs, which discharges three hundred thousand gallons of water per day, for the price of $2,500. The pump house and waterworks were built in 1902 and began serving as the main water supply for the growing city of Gainesville. This investment paid great dividends in 1905, when the University of Florida selected Gainesville as its location because the city was able to promise free water service to the campus through the recently constructed facility at Boulware Springs. Though the waterworks were shut down in 1948, the university receives free water service from the city to this day.

THE DUDLEY FARM

The small town of Newberry, located fifteen miles west of Gainesville, began as a mining town after phosphate was discovered there in 1889. The Savannah, Florida and Western Railway extended its tracks southward through the phosphate-producing territory in 1893 with a stop in Newberry. A post office established in March 1894 was named Newton, but changed to Newberry in August of that year as many of the area's new residents came from Newberry, South Carolina. By 1896, there were fourteen mines operating in the area, which led to the construction of hotels, boardinghouses and saloons to accommodate the mineworkers. In 1914, war was declared against Germany—the principal customer for Newberry's phosphate—and the local residents turned to farming as their primary source of income.

Located on Newberry Road, the Dudley Farm was owned and operated by the Dudley family for three generations. The first three hundred acres of land were originally purchased by Captain Phillip Benjamin Harvey Dudley in 1859. Captain Dudley and his wife, Mary Magdelina Thomson, had seven children, though only five survived to adulthood. On their land, the family raised cattle, hogs and turkeys and grew vegetables, cotton and sugar cane for the production of cane syrup.

After the Civil War, his son Phillip Benjamin Harvey Dudley Jr. would further develop the farm until it totaled more than six hundred acres. He also opened a general store and post office, making the crossroads that lead to the Dudley Farm the center of its community. In fact, during the 1870s,

Above: The Dudley Farm House as it appeared around 1910. *Courtesy of State Archives of Florida, Florida Memory, http://floridamemory.com/items/show/145203.*

Right: "Protection," from the First Coast Reflections project, Dudley Farm. *Author's original image.*

the Dudley Farm was larger than the city of Gainesville and was the area's second-largest employer after phosphate mining.

Myrtle Dudley, the youngest of Phillip Benjamin Harvey Dudley Jr.'s twelve children, donated the property to the Florida Park Service in 1983 to ensure that her mother's wishes that the farm be preserved forever would be carried out.

Today, the 325-acre farm includes eighteen authentic yellow-pine buildings counting the farmhouse, which still contains the original furnishings, and a working cane-syrup house. Among the livestock on the farm are Cracker cattle, one of the oldest and rarest breeds in the United States. The colorful cattle are descendants of the criollo cattle brought from Spain by the conquistadors.

The Dudley Farm Historic State Park, which is listed in the National Register of Historic Places and has been designated as a Florida Heritage Landmark, is open to visitors from 9:00 a.m. until 5:00 p.m. Wednesdays through Sundays. Special events hosted on the farm, such as the annual Quilt Day held in October and Cane Day held in December, are listed on the park's website.

THE MARJORIE KINNAN RAWLINGS HOUSE

Marjorie Kinnan Rawlings was born in Washington, D.C., and began writing at the age of six. She attended the University of Wisconsin–Madison, where she met a fellow writer, Charles Rawlings. They married in 1919 and moved to Louisville, Kentucky, and later to Rochester, New York, where they both wrote for the *Rochester Journal*. Charles's brothers, who were living in Island Grove and involved in real estate speculation, suggested that they consider moving to the area.

Cross Creek is located just west of the First Coast area in Alachua County, between the Lochloosa and Orange Lakes. A very rural area even now, Cross Creek was a remote wilderness area at the time, and its inhabitants were known as "Florida Crackers"—a term then applied to the Florida frontier settlers.

Following his brothers' suggestion, Charles and Marjorie came to Cross Creek in 1928. Their plan was to purchase the small house and its seventy-two acres of orange groves with money inherited from her mother's estate, make the majority of their income off the grove and write full time. They soon discovered that the inheritance merely provided them with a down payment, and they were forced to take out a mortgage although they both were unemployed at the time.

Having inherited her father's love of nature during summers spent on the family's Maryland farm, Marjorie adapted well to life in Cross Creek. She learned to hunt, fish, identify native flora and fauna and survive on her own in the wilderness. As her affection for the rural lifestyle increased, so did her disliking of cities, as evidenced by an excerpt from a 1938 sonnet published in *Scribner's*:

Now, having left cities behind me, turned
Away forever from the strange, gregarious
Huddling of men by stones, I find those various
Great towns I knew fused into one, burned
Together in the fire of my despising…[55]

The eight-room Florida Cracker–style house, believed to have been built in 1884, consists of three attached buildings constructed of cypress and heart pine. Typical of Cracker design and construction, the house has a ten-foot-high roof structure that allows the summer heat to rise and is raised off the ground by piers that provide for air circulation under the structure to help keep it cool. The structure also includes numerous windows for cross ventilation and a large covered front porch.

When Marjorie first purchased the home, it was unpainted. This was common practice in the area because heart pine is so dense with resin that paint tends to peel. The house also had no indoor plumbing, so she had the first indoor bathroom in all of Cross Creek installed. Marjorie then hosted a party in her new bathroom, complete with drinks served from a bathtub filled with ice and fresh flowers occupying the bowl of her new toilet. She also had the upper half of a small closet in the living room converted into a liquor cabinet.

In the kitchen is the wood-burning stove where Marjorie displayed her exceptional cooking skills when entertaining guests. In fact, she was such a good cook that she authored a most unique cookbook entitled *Cross Creek Cookery*, which includes such unusual recipes as swamp cabbage, alligator tail and pot roast of bear. She provided her readers with a variety of interesting and unusual anecdotes to complement the recipes, such as her observation that bears were becoming scarce in the area and that she could "see no reason for destroying the remaining ones" and that "a male bear in mating season, like a boar hog, is not fit to eat." But she also admitted that "bear meat at the proper season, and properly cooked, is a delicious meat."[56] She compares the meat of an alligator tail to that of liver or veal. She warns it must be cooked either very quickly or for a very long time to avoid toughness.

Also included were much less unusual recipes, such as her special recipe for "Black Bottom Pie," which she created by combining two recipes sent to her by friends, resulting in a pie she described as being "so delicate, so

Above: A vintage image of the Marjorie Kinnan Rawlings House; exact date of photograph unknown. *Courtesy of the Library of Congress Prints and Photographs Division, Washington, D.C.*

Right: The living room in the Marjorie Kinnan Rawlings House. Note the coat closet, which she had converted into a liquor cabinet. *Author's original image.*

luscious, that I hope to be propped up on my dying bed and fed a generous portion. Then I think that I should refuse outright to die, for life would be too good to relinquish."[57]

While she thrived and her writing flourished at Cross Creek, rural life was not to her husband's liking, and her already-troubled marriage to Charles Rawlings ended in divorce five years later. Marjorie suddenly found herself alone and responsible for paying the mortgage on her own.

Although she had experienced a certain level of success as a writer for the *Louisville Courier-Journal* while living in Kentucky and for the *Rochester Journal* while living in New York, Rawlings found new inspiration in her quiet, rural surroundings. Most of her writing was done at a small table on her screened-in porch, though she twice contracted malaria after arriving in the Cross Creek area and wrote from her bed while recovering. Her short stories were being published in national magazines, and her first novel, *South Moon Under*, was published in 1933. It beautifully illustrated her rediscovered relationship with nature and her appreciation of the solitude she found in the wilderness that she now called home, with phrases such as "The silence of the scrub was primordial. The wood-thrush crying across it might have been the first bird in the world—or the last."[58]

It was during her time at Cross Creek in 1938 that Marjorie Kinnan Rawlings wrote the Pulitzer Prize–winning and much-beloved story of a young boy and his pet deer, *The Yearling*. Today, more than seventy-five years after its initial publication, the story continues to touch the hearts of readers, young and old alike, with its moving depictions of life, love and difficult choices, as illustrated by this timelessly eloquent quote: "He lay down beside the fawn. He put one arm across its neck. It did not seem to him that he could ever be lonely again."[59]

In her book *Cross Creek*, Marjorie wrote of her love for the land that she had come to call her home with these words:

> *It seems to me that the earth may be borrowed but not bought. It may be used, but not owned…We are tenants and not possessors, lovers and not masters. Cross Creek belongs to the wind and the rain, to the sun and the seasons, to the cosmic secrecy of seed, and beyond all, to time.*[60]

It is only by visiting the site of her home that one can truly appreciate the sentiment of her words. She sought to share her love of the area with her frequent visitors, some of whom included artist N.C. Wyeth, fellow author Margaret Mitchell and poet Robert Frost, with whom she developed a deep

Marjorie Kinnan Rawlings on the front porch of her Cross Creek home in 1938. Photo by Alan Anderson. *Courtesy of the Marjorie Kinnan Rawlings Papers, Special and Area Studies Collections, George A. Smathers Libraries, University of Florida, Gainesville, Florida.*

friendship. It has been noted that Rawlings and Frost would read to each other after dinner and then sit by the fire in her living room, talking for hours. Actor Gregory Peck also stayed in Marjorie's home during the filming of the outdoor scenes of the 1946 movie version of *The Yearling*.

The simple board-and-batten house located on a small county road continued to be her only home until her marriage to Norton Baskin in 1941. After they married, Marjorie divided her time between Cross Creek, their home in Crescent Beach and Baskin's St. Augustine Castle Warden Hotel, a beautiful Moorish Revival building that is now the site of Ripley's Believe It or Not Museum. She purchased the Crescent Beach house from the owner of Marineland and enlarged it by adding an office after the film version of *The Yearling* was released. At the beach house, she entertained guests such as Ernest Hemingway, Zora Neale Hurston and Dylan Thomas.

Yet, even after her marriage and her success as a writer, Marjorie continued to worry about her finances. In a 1943 letter to Baskin, she confided that she continued "to have nightmares of homelessness."[61] Although she is often remembered as a strong-willed and independent woman, Norton Baskin is quoted as having said, after seeing the 1983 film version of *Cross Creek*, that:

> *In the movie, they portrayed Marjorie as strong and independent. And she was, absolutely. But at speaking engagements, she would say, "Don't you leave me." She was one of the shyest people I've ever seen. She needed somebody to lean on.*[62]

In fact, many have noted that Marjorie was a complicated woman. She was noted, by those who knew her well, for her kindness and generosity but also for her impatience and moodiness. Although she loved the rural lifestyle in Cross Creek, she was well ahead of her time when it came to her feelings on race relations. She insisted that her maid, an African American woman named Idella Parker, always ride beside her in the front seat of her car. She also took Idella to see a film in an Ocala "whites only" theater, verbally abusing the doorman until they both were allowed inside.

Marjorie Kinnan Rawlings died of a cerebral hemorrhage at her Crescent Beach cottage in 1953 at the age of fifty-seven. She is buried at the Antioch Cemetery near Island Grove, about seven miles east of her home at Cross Creek. Beside her rests her husband, Norton Baskin, who died in 1997. Her grave marker bears this inscription, which was written by her husband: "Through her writing she endeared herself to the people of the world." At the head of her grave marker, an unknown visitor has placed three statues of a buck, a doe and a fawn, all lying down with their legs folded underneath their bodies, peacefully resting together.

In her will, Rawlings left her beloved Cross Creek home to the University of Florida, where she had taught creative writing. When the university announced

Marjorie's Room, from the First Coast Reflections project, Marjorie Kinnan Rawlings House. *Author's original image.*

its plan to use the property as a writers' retreat, Norton Baskin put all of Marjorie's Cross Creek home furnishings and possessions into storage to preserve them for future generations. All of the items remained in storage until 1970, when the home was acquired by the Florida Division of Recreation and Parks to become the Marjorie Kinnan Rawlings Historic State Park. Norton Baskin then released the items from storage and had them returned and reinstalled at the house, so that visitors could experience the home exactly as it was when Marjorie lived there. Most of the furnishings and artwork on display in the house are original; their placement is based on historical photographs.

Listed in the National Register of Historic Places, designated as a National Historic Landmark and a Florida Heritage Landmark, Marjorie's Cross Creek home is now part of the Florida State Parks system. To find the park, take U.S. Highway 301 south out of Hawthorne (for ten miles) to County Road 325; then head west for approximately four miles. Guided house tours at the Marjorie Kinnan Rawlings Historic State Park are available Thursdays through Sundays, although the farmyard, groves and trails are open daily.

Afterword

Too often we see history as a boring recitation of names, dates and places related to major events on a national or international basis. It is my hope that through this book, I am able to share my personal belief that history is so much more than that.

I believe that history was not only made on the battlefields but also in the kitchens of simple homesteads and the fields of rural farms. I believe that it was not only sacrifices of the generals and the foot soldiers that created the cities we now call our homes but also the everyday efforts of the countless individuals who had the courage to endure and overcome adversity and the initiative to establish communities where there previously were none.

I further believe that the great works of art, created by people who were carving out their existence under unfamiliar and sometimes-difficult circumstances, serve as an enduring testament to the fact that what is essentially an individual experience can be transformed into something that can easily be universally appreciated. This belief is evidenced by the fact that *The Florida Suite* has been applauded by audiences worldwide and *The Yearling* has been translated into twenty-nine languages and read by literally millions around the world.

Finally, I believe that the preservation and restoration of homes such as the ones featured in this book are vital to our understanding of the past and profoundly impact how we make the decisions that will shape our futures, both as individuals and as communities.

It is my sincere hope that by sharing my discoveries with those who read this book, I might, in some small way, contribute to the efforts to preserve and restore the historic homes of Florida's First Coast.

ADDITIONAL INFORMATION

Visitors to Florida's First Coast area may contact the following for additional information on historic sites:

Visit Jacksonville
208 North Laura Street, Suite 102
Jacksonville, FL 32202
(800) 733-2668 (U.S. and Canada)
www.visitjacksonville.com

Beaches Visitor Center
380 Pablo Avenue
Jacksonville Beach, FL 32250
(904) 242-0024
www.visitjacksonville.com

St. Augustine and St. Johns County Visitor Information Center
10 South Castillo Drive
St. Augustine, FL 32084
(904) 825-1000
www.floridashistoriccoast.com

For further information on the locations featured in this book, please contact the following organizations:

Kingsley Plantation
United States National Park Service
11676 Palmetto Avenue
Jacksonville, FL 32226
(904) 251-3537
www.nps.gov/timu/historyculture/kp.htm

The Major Webb House
Mandarin Museum and Historical Society
11964 Mandarin Road
Jacksonville, FL 32223
(904) 268-0784
www.mandarinmuseum.net

The Delius House
Jacksonville Historical Society
317 A. Philip Randolph Boulevard
Jacksonville, FL 32202
(904) 665-0064
www.jaxhistory.com

The Merrill House
Jacksonville Historical Society
317 A. Philip Randolph Boulevard
Jacksonville, FL 32202
(904) 665-0064
www.jaxhistory.com

The Foreman's House
Beaches Area Historical Society
381 Beach Boulevard
Jacksonville Beach, FL 32250
(904) 241-5657
www.beachesmuseum.org

The González-Alvarez House
St. Augustine Historical Society
271 Charlotte Street
St. Augustine, FL 32084
(904) 824-2872
www.staugustinehistoricalsociety.org

The Father O'Reilly House
Sisters of St. Joseph
32 Aviles Street
St. Augustine, FL 32084
(904) 826-0750
www.oreillyhouse.org.

The Tovar House
St. Augustine Historical Society
271 Charlotte Street
St. Augustine, FL 32084
(904) 824-2872
www.staugustinehistoricalsociety.org

The Peña-Peck House
Woman's Exchange of St. Augustine
143 St. George Street
St. Augustine, FL 32084
(904) 829-5046
www.penapeckhouse.com

The Fernandez-Llambias House
St. Augustine Historical Society
271 Charlotte Street
St. Augustine, FL 32084
(904) 824-2872
www.staugustinehistoricalsociety.org

The Ximenez-Fatio House
National Society of the Colonial Dames of America in the State of Florida
28 Cadiz Street
St. Augustine, FL 32084
(904) 829-3575
www.ximenezfatiohouse.org

The Prince Murat House
Dow Museum of Historic Houses
149 Cordova Street
St. Augustine, FL 32084
(904) 823-9722
www.moas.org/dowmuseum.html

The Dow House
Dow Museum of Historic Houses
149 Cordova Street
St. Augustine, FL 32084
(904) 823-9722
www.moas.org/dowmuseum.html

The Canova-de Medicis House
Dow Museum of Historic Houses
149 Cordova Street
St. Augustine, FL 32084
(904) 823-9722
www.moas.org/dowmuseum.html

The Howells House
Dow Museum of Historic Houses
149 Cordova Street
St. Augustine, FL 32084
(904) 823-9722
www.moas.org/dowmuseum.html

The Spear House
Dow Museum of Historic Houses
149 Cordova Street
St. Augustine, FL 32084
(904) 823-9722
www.moas.org/dowmuseum.html

The Rose House
Dow Museum of Historic Houses
149 Cordova Street
St. Augustine, FL 32084
(904) 823-9722
www.moas.org/dowmuseum.html

The Worcester House
Dow Museum of Historic Houses
149 Cordova Street
St. Augustine, FL 32084
(904) 823-9722
www.moas.org/dowmuseum.html

The Carpenter's House
Dow Museum of Historic Houses
149 Cordova Street
St. Augustine, FL 32084
(904) 823-9722
www.moas.org/dowmuseum.html

The Clarke House
Historical Society of Orange Park, Inc.
P.O. Box 08
Orange Park, FL 32067
www.ophistory.org

Dudley Farm Historic State Park
Florida State Parks
18730 West Newberry Road
Newberry, FL 32669
(352) 472-1142
www.floridastateparks.org/DudleyFarm

Marjorie Kinnan Rawlings Historic State Park
Florida State Parks
18700 South County Road 325
Cross Creek, FL 32640
(352) 466-3672
www.floridastateparks.org/marjoriekinnanrawlings

NOTES

1. Laudonnière, *Three Voyages*, 186.
2. Ibid., 162.
3. Bennett, *Laudonnière and Fort Caroline*, 39.
4. Laudonnière, *Three Voyages*, 165.
5. "Floripedia: De Gourgues, Dominique."
6. Bartram, *Travels*, 81.
7. Bartram, *Travels*; "St. Johns River Timeline."
8. Bartram, *Travels*, 82.
9. Ward, *Old Hickory's Town*, 139.
10. Dykes letter.
11. Spencer, *Greetings from Florida*, 27.
12. Barbour, *Florida for Tourists, Invalids, and Settlers*, 94.
13. Crooks, *Jacksonville After the Fire*, 17.
14. Dr. Bronson's History, Jacksonville.
15. Hallock, *Camp Life in Florida*, 176.
16. National Park Service, "Kingsley Plantation, Drawings," Sheet 1.
17. Schafer, *Anna Kingsley*, 32.
18. Kingsley, *Treatise*.
19. Landers, *Colonial Plantations*, 108.
20. Schafer, *Anna Madgigine Jai Kingsley*, 43.
21. Ibid., 43.
22. Bartram, *Travels*, 83.
23. Stowe, Harriet Beecher. *Palmetto Leaves*. Gainesville: University Press of Florida, 1999. Page 247.

24. Graff, *Mandarin on the St. Johns*, 62.
25. "Fruit Trees Popped."
26. Graff, *Mandarin on the St. Johns*, 61.
27. Richmond, *Solano Grove Rediscovered*, 3–5.
28. Gillispie, "Search for Thomas F. Ward."
29. Fenby, *On Delius in Florida*, 5.
30. Arntz, *Frederick Delius in Florida*.
31. Richmond, *Solano Grove Rediscovered*, 3–5.
32. "Buried Treasure, Part 2."
33. "Early Florida East Coast Railway."
34. Garner letter.
35. Grajales, *The Founding of St. Augustine*.
36. Barrientos, *Pedro Menéndez de Avilés*, 106.
37. Porter, *John James Audubon*, 9.
38. Ibid., 12.
39. Emerson, *Poetry Notebooks*, 7.
40. Waterbury, *Treasurer's House*, 81.
41. National Park Service, *Tovar "Cannonball" House*, 4.
42. Waterbury, *Treasurer's House*, 199.
43. Burbey, *Our Worthy Commander*.
44. Waterbury, Jean Parker. *Many Lives*, 24–25.
45. Bartram, *Travels*, 457–58.
46. Emerson, *Early Poems*, xvi.
47. United States Supreme Court, *Colin Mitchell and Others v. United States*.
48. St. Johns County, Records, Deed Book "Q," 422.
49. McGuire, *Howells the Nomad*, 21.
50. Howells, "Confession of St. Augustine," 883.
51. Ibid., 686
52. Hall, *St. Augustine*, 76.
53. Howells, "Home-Towners," 86.
54. Gordon, *Pageant of the Rose*, 80.
55. Rawlings, *Having Left Cities Behind Me*.
56. Rawlings, *Cross Creek Cookery*, 110.
57. Ibid., 174.
58. Rawlings, *South Moon Under*, 119.
59. Rawlings, *Yearling*, 202.
60. Rawlings, *Cross Creek*, 380.
61. Rawlings Papers.
62. Flood, "Man At Cross Creek."

BIBLIOGRAPHY

Arntz, James. *Frederick Delius in Florida: A Music-Performance Documentary Film for Public Television.* Produced and written by James Arntz. PBS, 2009.

Barbour, George M. *Florida for Tourists, Invalids, and Settlers.* New York: D. Appleton and Company, 1881.

Barrientos, Bartolome. *Pedro Menéndez de Avilés: Founder of Florida.* Gainesville: University of Florida Press, 1965.

Bartram, William. *Travels and Other Writings.* New York: Literary Classics of the United States, 1996.

Bennett, Charles. *Laudonnière and Fort Caroline.* Tuscaloosa: University of Alabama Press, 2001.

Burbey, Louis. *Our Worthy Commander: the Life and Times of Benjamin K. Pierce, in Whose Honor Fort Pierce Was Named.* Fort Pierce: Indian River Community College Historical, 1976.

"Buried Treasure, Part 2." *Florida Times Union* (Jacksonville), August 22, 1999.

Burt, Al. *The Tropic of Cracker.* Gainesville: University Press of Florida, 1999.

Crooks, James B. *Jacksonville After the Fire.* Jacksonville: University of North Florida Press, 1991.

Davis, T. Frederick. *History of Jacksonville, Florida and Vicinity: 1513 to 1924.* St. Augustine: Florida Historical Society, 1925.

Dykes, Jasper Jackson. "Jasper Jackson Dykes Letter." Sons of Confederate Veterans, Florida Division. http://www.florida-scv.org/Camp1360/jasper_dykes_letter.htm (accessed June 14, 2014).

"Early Florida East Coast Railway." Dr. Bronson's History. http://www.drbronsontours.com/bronsonfloridaeastcoastrailwayinformation.html. (accessed July 22, 2014).

Emerson, Ralph Waldo. *The Early Poems of Ralph Waldo Emerson, with an introduction by Nathan Haskell Dole*. New York: T.Y. Crowell, 1899.

———. *The Poetry Notebooks of Ralph Waldo Emerson*. Kansas City: University of Missouri Press, 1986.

Fenby, Eric. *On Delius in Florida*. Program note. Jacksonville, FL: Annual Delius Festival, March 7–10, 1984.

Flood, Danielle. "The Man At Cross Creek It Wasn't Easy Being Marred To Marjorie Kinnan Rawlings. Just Ask Her Husband—Whose Story Isn't In Any Book Or Movie." *Sun-Sentinel*, September 8, 1985. http://articles.sun-sentinel.com/1985-09-08/features/8502070560_1_marjorie-kinnan-rawlings-creek-movie/2 (accessed June 25, 2014).

"Floripedia: De Gourgues, Dominque." Exploring Florida. http://fcit.usf.edu/florida/docs/d/degour.htm (accessed July 21, 2014).

"Fruit Trees Popped Like Pistols During 1894–95 Great Freeze." *Orlando Sentinel*, May 20, 1988. http://articles.orlandosentinel.com/1998-05-20/features/9805150662_1_great-freeze-sanford-trees (accessed June 3, 2014).

Garner, Jim. Letter written to the Beaches Area Historical Society by former Seaboard Air Line Railroad employee. Jacksonville Beach, n.d.

Gillispie, Don C. "The Search for Thomas F. Ward, Delius' Teacher." http://www.thebluegrassspecial.com/archive/2011/june2011/classical-perspectives.html (accessed June 20, 2014).

Gordon, Jean. *Pageant of the Rose*. New York: Studio Publications, 1953.

Graff, Mary B. *Mandarin on the St. Johns*. Gainesville: University of Florida Press, 1953.

Graham, Thomas. *Flagler's St. Augustine Hotels*. Sarasota: Pineapple Press, 2004.

Grajales, Francisco Lopez de Mendoza. *Founding of St. Augustine*. Early Americas Digital Archive. http://mith.umd.edu//eada/html/display.php?docs=lopez_de_mendoza_staugustine.xml&action=show (accessed June 21, 2014).

Hall, Maggi Smith. *St. Augustine*. Charleston, SC: Arcadia Publishing, 2002.

Hallock, Charles. *Camp Life in Florida; A Handbook for Sportsmen and Settlers*. New York: Forest and Stream Publishing Company, 1876.

Hooper, Kevin S. *The Early History of Clay County: A Wilderness That Could Be Tamed*. Charleston, SC: The History Press, 2006.

Howells, William Dean. "A Confession of St. Augustine." *Harper's Magazine* vol. 134 (May 1916 to May 1917): 883.

———. "The Home-Towners." *El Escribano: The St. Augustine Journal of History* (1998): 88.

"Jacksonville." Dr. Bronson's History. http://www.drbronsontours.com/ bronsonjacksonville.html (accessed June 7, 2014).

Kingsley, Zephaniah Jr. *A Treatise on the Patriarchal System of Society.* 1828. Timucuan Ecological and Historic Preserve. http://www.nps.gov/timu/ historyculture/kp_zk_treatise.htm (accessed May 23, 2014).

Landers, Jane L. *Colonial Plantations and Economy in Florida.* Gainesville: University Press of Florida, 2000.

Laudonnière, René Goulaine de. *Three Voyages, translated by Charles Bennett.* Tuscaloosa: University of Alabama Press, 2001.

Manucy, Albert C. *Houses of St. Augustine, 1565–1821.* Gainesville: University Press of Florida, 1991.

———. *Sixteenth-Century St. Augustine: The People and Their Homes.* Gainesville: University Press of Florida, 1997.

McGrath, John. *The French in Early Florida: In the Eye of the Hurricane.* Gainesville: University Press of Florida, 2000.

McGuire, William. *Howells the Nomad.* St. Augustine, FL: El Escribano, 1998.

Mueller, Edward A. *First Coast Steamboat Days.* Jacksonville, FL: Jacksonville Historical Society, 2005.

———. *Steamboating on the St. Johns.* Melbourne, FL: South Brevard Historical Society, 1980.

———. *Steamships of the Two Henrys: Being an Account of the Maritime Activities of Henry Morrison Flagler and Henry Bradley Plant.* Jacksonville, FL: Edward A. Mueller, 1996.

Murray, Nancy H. *The Madonnas of St. Augustine: A Remarkable History.* Jacksonville, FL: Hart Street Publishers, 2013.

National Park Service. "Kingsley Plantation, Drawings." Historic American Buildings Survey, 2005.

———. *Tovar "Cannonball" House.* HABS No. FLA-140. Historic American Buildings Survey, n.d.

Nolan, David, *The Houses of St. Augustine.* Sarasota, FL: Pineapple Press, 1995.

Porter, Charlotte M. *John James Audubon: Florida Travels.* Daytona, FL: Museum of Arts and Sciences, 1999.

Rawlings, Marjorie Kinnan. *Cross Creek.* New York: Touchstone, 1996.

———. *Cross Creek Cookery.* New York: Simon and Schuster, Fireside Edition, 1996.

————. *Having Left Cities Behind Me*. New York: Charles Scribner's Sons, 1938.

————. Letter by Marjorie Kinnan Rawlings to Norton Baskin. Marjorie Kinnan Rawlings Papers; Series 1: Correspondence. TLS to NB. 4 p. September 23, 1943 [Crescent Beach] Smathers Library, University of Florida. http://web.uflib.ufl.edu/spec/manuscript/rawlings/rawlings2.htm#section-21 (accessed July 18, 2014).

————. *South Moon Under*. Dunwoody, GA: Norman S. Berg, 1977.

————. *The Yearling*. New York: Scribner Paperback Edition, 2002.

Reynolds, Charles B. *Old St. Augustine: A Story of Three Centuries*. St. Augustine, FL: E.H. Reynolds, 1886.

Richmond, Martha Bullard. "Solano Grove Rediscovered: A Personal Account." *Delius Society Journal* 82 (April 1984): 3–5.

Rogers, Debra Webb. *San Marco*. Charleston, SC: Arcadia Publishing, 2010.

Rogers, Rebecca Yerkes, and Robert W. Harper III. *The Ximenez-Fatio House Museum*. St. Augustine: Florida State Museum House of the National Society of the Colonial Dames of America in the State of Florida, 2012.

Schafer, Daniel L. *Anna Kingsley*. St. Augustine: St. Augustine Historical Society, 1994.

————. *Anna Madgigine Jai Kingsley: African Princess, Florida Slave, Plantation Owner*. Gainesville: University Press of Florida, 2003.

————. *William Bartram and the Ghost Plantations of East Florida*. Gainesville: University Press of Florida, 2010.

Spencer, Donald D. *Greetings from Jacksonville*. Atglen, PA: Schiffer Publishing, 2008.

St. Johns County. Records, Deed Book "Q."

"St. Johns River Timeline." St. Johns Riverkeeper. http://www.stjohnsriverkeeper.org/the-river/history (accessed July 12, 2014).

United States Supreme Court. *Colin Mitchell and Others v. United States*. January, 1831.

Ward, James Robertson. *Old Hickory's Town: An Illustrated History of Jacksonville*. Jacksonville: Florida Publishing Company, 1982.

Waterbury, Jean Parker. *The Gonzales-Alvarez Oldest House: The Place and Its People*. St. Augustine, FL: St. Augustine Historical Society, 1984.

————. *The Many Lives of the Llambias House*. St. Augustine, FL: St. Augustine Historical Society, 1997.

————. *The Treasurer's House*. St. Augustine, FL: St. Augustine Historical Society, 1994.

————. *The Ximenez-Fatio House "Long Neglected, Now Restored."* St. Augustine, FL: St. Augustine Historical Society, 1995.

Wood, Dr. Wayne W. *Jacksonville's Architectural Heritage*. Gainesville: University Press of Florida, 1989.

Wynne, Lewis Nicholas. *Florida in the Civil War*. Charleston, SC: Arcadia Publishing, 2003.

INDEX

ABOUT THE AUTHORS

Author and artist Mary Atwood is a long-time resident of the First Coast area whose deep appreciation of its natural beauty, rich history and diverse culture is often reflected in her work. Ms. Atwood's close connections to and collaborative efforts with local historical societies provide unique opportunities for her to capture, in both words and images, the stories associated with house museums throughout the First Coast area. Her fine art photography has won numerous awards and has been exhibited internationally. To learn more about Mary's photography, please visit her website at www. MaryAtwoodPhotoArt.com.

William Weeks is a graduate of Florida State University, where he majored in creative writing. He has applied his writing skills to a variety of venues from instructional design and corporate training to spoken word and theater. A lifelong resident of the area, he has enjoyed being a part of the writing of *Historic Homes of Florida's First Coast*. William is also a blogger and can be found online at www.catzenspace.com.

Often called "the undisputed godfather of preservation in Northeast Florida," Dr. Wayne Wood is the founder of Riverside Avondale Preservation, Inc., one of the largest neighborhood preservation groups in the South. He is also the founder of the Riverside Arts Market, which is Florida's largest free weekly arts and entertainment venue. He has published fourteen books on architecture and history. Retired after many decades as an optometrist, Wayne now lists his profession as "arts agitator."